D1260793

Forgotten Hero:
General James B. McPherson

Forgotten Hero:
GENERAL JAMES B. McPHERSON

The Biography of a Civil War General

ELIZABETH J. WHALEY

EXPOSITION PRESS • NEW YORK

FIRST EDITION

Published by the Exposition Press Inc.
386 Fourth Avenue, New York 16, N.Y.
Designed by Morry M. Gropper
Manufactured in the United States of America
Consolidated Book Producers, Inc.
Library of Congress catalog card number: 54-11323

TO MY MOTHER

Preface

This book is the story of a man and a soldier whose name and accomplishments during the Civil War appeared on the pages of every newspaper and were known to every American.

Beloved of Grant, intimate of Sherman, idol of his army, Major General James B. McPherson made a meteoric rise to fame almost unparalleled in American history. His untimely death before Atlanta cut off a career that many military men and civilians predicted would carry him to the White House. He was the highest-ranking officer and the only army commander in the Federal forces killed in the great war.

Through the irony of fate, few historians of today make mention of his name, and Americans as a whole have never heard it.

In presenting this story of his life, I have tried to bring out of the shadows of forgetfulness a figure who left a permanent mark on the history of his country; an officer whose dynamic personality was reflected in the results of many engagements on the battlefield; a gentleman whose talent for friendship and love for people endeared him to thousands; a leader whose quick decisions and wise, cool judgments were needed after the noise of battle had subsided.

The history of the Reconstruction period would make happier reading if McPherson's hand could have guided the ship of state during that stormy time.

E. J. W.

Acknowledgments

Grateful acknowledgment is made for permission to quote from published works—

To D. Appleton-Century Company for *Battles and Leaders of the Civil War* and for the *Memoirs of General W. T. Sherman.*

To the *Clyde Enterprise* for material on General James B. McPherson.

To the Houghton Mifflin Company for John Fiske's *The Mississippi Valley in the Civil War,* and for Amelia Neville's *The Fantastic City.*

To the Ohio State Archaeological and Historical Society (Ohio State Museum) for the *Diary and Letters of Rutherford B. Hayes* (ed. Charles Richard Williams).

To William Sloane Associates, Inc., for Fletcher Pratt's *Ordeal by Fire.*

Thanks are also due to Eula McConnell Baumann, who furnished data relating to the members of the McPherson and Russell families in Clyde, Ohio; also, memoranda of the activities of Major General McPherson during the Civil War and events following his death.

Much of this material is in a scrapbook of newspaper clippings that evidently had been saved by her grandmother, Emeline McPherson Vandercook, the general's only sister.

We also thank Jean Hitchcolk Scrogin of Miami, Florida, a member of the McPherson family, who gave important data on the McPherson genealogy. After extensive research, particularly in New York and Pennsylvania, she was able to trace the movements of the several McPherson brothers and their children, who came at different times from Scotland to America.

To the many others who told something concerning the people and the happenings of the early days in Clyde, we are grateful.

E. J. W.

Contents

Forgotten Hero:
General James B. McPherson

CHAPTER I

Seeking New Land

It was a bright April day in northern Ohio in 1823. The waters of Lake Erie reflected the blueness of the sky, and the little waves glittered and danced as they tried to climb the long stretches of sandy beach. A short distance from the shore began those vast forests of elm, maple, beech, walnut and other trees that almost covered the great state, proving the excellence of the soil.

Ohio was young and wild. Her taming had but recently started. Scarcely more than a quarter of a century had elapsed since that part of the state had received its first white settlers. Cleveland, first surveyed in 1796, was now a growing town of nearly a thousand inhabitants. Norwalk had many Revolutionary families from Connecticut who had made homes in the Firelands. Portland, now Sandusky, invited settlers with its wide protected bay. Lower Sandusky, now Fremont, had acquired new families since Croghan's dramatic repulse of the enemy in the War of 1812. The eyes of all the eastern states were turned westward. Ohio was attracting home-seekers, explorers, businessmen, adventurers.

In 1820, three years before this story opens, northwestern Ohio had been opened to settlement by Congress. In the same year, Sandusky County had been organized, with Lower Sandusky its county seat.

On that April day five men might be seen walking westward on the lake trail. These men, William McPherson, Norton Russell, James Birdseye and his son Nathan, and Lyman Babcock, had left Hopewell, Ontario County, New York, attracted by the accounts that had reached them concerning the Ohio country. They had walked to Buffalo and there had engaged passage on a small boat bound for Cleveland. Each had enough money on his person to purchase at least sixty acres of land at $1.25 per acre. William McPherson, who was always conscious of his hoarded savings, became suspicious of the boat's crew. He whispered to Birdseye, "James, I don't like the looks of yonder 'hawkeye.' We'd do well to get off."

Responded James, "I agree with you. I've not seen such a villainous face in all of York State."

They whispered their fears to their companions, and all decided to disembark at Ashtabula and walk the remaining distance. They followed the girdled road into Cleveland, and were now trying to keep to the uncertain trail made by the Indians. They were in high spirits, for all, except James Birdseye, were young and were now entering upon a great adventure. They had with them some of the food needed, and their squirrel rifles offered them a means of getting fresh meat every day. They studied the plant life as they walked, and discussed the fertility of the soil.

James Birdseye could see that there would be a road along the lake some day. He had made many roads in western New York and became known as "Turnpike Birdseye." His two main objects in coming to Ohio were to help build the roads, and to acquire lands from the government in payment for his services as he had in New York.

When these men reached Huron they turned south on the trail to Norwalk, then west on the "horseback mail route," a trail through the woods that led to Lower Sandusky.

They came to Amsden's Corners (now Bellevue), which consisted of a crossroad and two log cabins, one vacant and the other occupied by Isaac Amsden, who had on sale a few articles needed by the early settlers. After a short rest in the vacant cabin, the travelers walked in a westerly direction until they came to the South Ridge; then in a north-westerly direction for over a mile until they reached the cabin of Seth Murry on the North Ridge. Murry was a neighbor from Hopewell who had preceded them by a few months. Here they made their home while they looked about for a location.

The land office was in Bucyrus; James Birdseye, taking each man's money, proceeded on foot by Indian trail to that place. He paid for the land and brought back the deeds. The men obtained the services of Sylvanus Bourne, surveyor for Greencreek Township, who marked the boundaries of their farms as described on the deeds. Each man took possession of his farm and began clearing a space to build a log cabin.[1]

William McPherson's Ancestry[2]

Three brothers of Scottish descent, born and bred in Scotland, left their homeland and settled in Ireland. Whether they came alone or with their parents is not known. They were of Protestant stock. Their names were William McPherson, Robert McPherson and John McPherson. Professor W. H. McIntosh's *History of Ontario County* states that John McPherson, upon arrival in this country, settled in Pennsylvania temporarily. But the land in New York, called the Genesee Country in that state, was then opening up to settlement and was attracting many families from the surrounding state. This book also states that John McPherson came to Easton Township in 1798. Undoubtedly, the three brothers arrived before that date, as it is known that William McPherson, son of John and Elizabeth McPherson, was born in Easton Township in 1796 (in what is now Hopewell Township). It is believed that John's wife, Elizabeth, was Irish, which might indicate they were married before coming to America. Robert died before September 8, 1800. William and John, with

[1] Notes are at the end of the book.

their families, are listed in the 1800 census for Ontario County, New York.

Records show that John and Elizabeth McPherson acquired a large tract of land in Hopewell Township; also that by 1810 they had ten children. John McPherson died on June 24, 1812, at the age of forty-six years. His second son, William, who was then sixteen years of age, went to live with a neighbor, James Birdseye, for his living expenses and a chance to learn the trade of blacksmith. He also worked about the farm and cared for the Birdseye horses. There was a picture showing William, with the horses, in the family of Nathan Birdseye, son of James. William must have been a successful blacksmith, for on December 15, 1819, when he was twenty-three years old, he was able to purchase for $150 a tract of land from James Birdseye.

It was about this time that William began courting Cynthia Russell, a neighbor girl who was born in Hopewell on September 11, 1805. She was the fourth child of John Russell and his wife Lydia. John Russell was born in New Canaan, Massachusetts in 1774. He married Lydia Norton, daughter of Abijah and Lucy Norton, who was born in Richmond, Massachusetts, November 28, 1777.

John Russell and Lydia Norton were married in 1798. In 1801 they moved to New York State in a sled drawn by a yoke of oxen and settled in Gorham Township, Ontario County. They had five children. The father died when Cynthia was eight years old, and she lived for some time with a family named Silsby between Bath and Horseheads, New York. Later the mother married James Chase, and Cynthia went back to Hopewell.

When Cynthia was seventeen years of age she and William McPherson became engaged; in making plans for their married life, they found that the rich lands of Ohio offered them the best place to locate. When William left Hopewell in the spring of 1823, it was the understanding that as soon as he could get his land and build a cabin, he would return and marry Cynthia and take her to their Ohio home.

William McPherson's farm of one hundred and sixty acres lay along the North Ridge, beginning about twenty-five rods northeast of the present corporation limits of Clyde on Route 101[3] It extended southwesterly on the ridge road to the "horseback mail route" (now Route 20), then east to approximately Church Street, and north to the ridge. McPherson built his cabin on the ridge trail opposite the barn on the Thomas Dunigan farm. He also built a smithy almost on the site of the barn. Both buildings faced the ridge trail, for Maple Street did not then exist.

William worked very hard clearing his land and getting his cabin in readiness. He made a table, a bed and two stools, which, together with the fireplace, constituted the standard equipment for most log cabins. He lived in his cabin and prepared his simple fare. In February, 1824, he returned to Hopewell, where, on the fourth of March, he and Cynthia were married. Because he could earn fairly good wages in New York that summer, they decided to stay there for a few months.

In August they began the journey to Ohio by walking to Buffalo. William was determined that Cynthia should travel by boat from Buffalo to Portland, though she protested she could walk the distance easily. The extra money he had earned during the summer allowed them the luxury of the boat ride, from which the young couple derived much pleasure. They walked the ridge trail from Portland to their cabin, a distance of nearly twenty miles, carrying the few articles they had brought with them—an iron kettle and a few dishes and some garden and flower seeds. Wrapped tightly around a pole which they carried between them were woolen blankets and clothing that Cynthia had spun and made. On her nineteenth birthday, September 11, 1824, William and Cynthia together entered the log cabin that was "home."

CHAPTER II

Hamer's Corners

In the year that followed, other people from the east took up claims on the North Ridge and other trails. McPherson and his widely separated neighbors began to realize that the ridge trail made a circuitous route to Stemtown and Bakertown. A direct road from McPherson to McMillan (at Maple and South streets) would save about two miles of travel.

In March, 1825, several men met at McPherson's cabin and drew up a petition to the county commissioners for permission to cut such a road. They were granted the right to do this, and immediately the men started to do the work under the direction of James Birdseye. Thus Maple Street was cut out of the forest, more than a fourth of it being on McPherson's land.[1]

> In the meantime the United States government saw the necessity of an east and west road in northern Ohio to accommodate the thousands of eastern people who wanted to get some of cheap lands to the west. So the Western Reserve and Maumee Turnpike were cut from the western line of Huron County to the Maumee River, south of Toledo. The work was given to several contractors. James Birdseye had charge of that part of the road from Amsden's Corners to Lower Sandusky. He

began in 1825 and finished in 1827, having built four toll gates between the two towns. He also constructed the first bridge over the ford in the Sandusky River, finishing in 1828 at the contract price of $3,000.[2]

McPherson saw that the intersection of the new turnpike with Maple Street would form a "corners" touching his land, and knew the advantage of owning the four corners. "In March, 1826, he purchased from Albert Guinall for $409.12 a tract of land of 102.28 acres that lay east of what he owned, some of it being south of the 'mail route'; he purchased in April, 1826, another ten acres from Guinall for $133. The latter tract consisted of the triangle bounded by Main Street, the Maumee Pike and Maple Street. It was on the latter piece of ground that the tavern was built a few years later by William Hamer who had purchased the triangle from McPherson for $150."[3] McPherson's profit of $17 was considered high finance at that time.

William McPherson was an ambitious man with the thrift of the Scot as well as that of the pioneer. He put all his faculties to work in order to succeed. He cleared the new land for corn and other crops, and planted apple and peach trees on the west bank of the ravine. The east bank and the bottom land along Buck Creek he used for pasture. He also continued the blacksmith trade, many times taking grain, hickory nuts, cornmeal or wool in exchange for his work, for money was scarce among the early settlers. He would then load his wagon with such commodities as he could spare and take them to Portland or to Lower Sandusky, where he could dispose of them to some trader for cash; or bargain them for something he needed; or for something he could dispose of at an advantage at the Corners. He thus became known as a successful farmer and a shrewd businessman.

Meanwhile, his wife's mother, Lydia Chase, became a widow in New York State and, in the fall of 1828, came to Hamer's Corners to make her home with her children, Cynthia, Norton and William, the latter having come to Ohio in 1825. She was with Cynthia, who gave birth to her first-born on November 14, 1828. She helped William keep the fire blazing and the house comfortable. She also tried to allay his extreme nervousness and the concern over his wife which most young husbands endure in the process of becoming a father for the first time. Cynthia's patience and fortitude were matched by those of her mother, who had given birth to six children.

When Cynthia received the beautiful baby boy her mother placed in her arms, her eyes held the look of love and wonder that all mothers show when the great miracle of life comes to pass. William could now talk more rationally, and kneeling at his wife's side, he uttered the name that both had hoped to give to their first-born, "James Birdseye McPherson."

On February 5, 1830, William and Cynthia became the parents of a daughter, whom they called Emeline. "In October of that year they sold to William Hamer the ten-acre triangle before mentioned; they also sold to him all of their land west of Maple Street consisting of 89.26 acres, for $460." Hamer immediately began the construction of a two-story log tavern on the highest point of the triangle. The place soon became known as Hamer's Corners. He also built a large frame house (the present Thomas Dunigan home) opposite the McPherson log cabin. In the winter of 1830-31 the McPherson home caught fire and burned to the ground. Hamer invited the McPhersons to move into his new house and they were glad to do so.

By this time the North Ridge Trail had become an artery of travel. Scarcely a day passed without the McPhersons noting several persons riding or walking by. It might be a neighbor stopping at William's smithy to have some nails made; perhaps a new family moving into the Corners, having just arrived from Portland; or a mill-owner or general-store operator from the Corners or from Stemtown going to Portland to get goods shipped there from Buffalo. In the spring, Indians passed by on their way from the Seneca Reservation, five miles south of the Corners, to Portland to get the annual bounty paid them by the United States Treasury in consideration of their giving up their lands in New York State to the government.

Some of these Indians had lived near the Birdseyes in that state. Tall Chief, whom William McPherson knew well, was one of the chiefs who came to Ohio. In the spring of 1830, when

James McPherson was about eighteen months old, Tall Chief stopped to visit his old friend, the baby's father. After fondling little James, Tall Chief looked at the mother and said, "Fine boy, fine boy! Be big man!" This prophetic remark pleased the mother at the time, and was recalled after the fall of Vicksburg.

In the summer of 1831 McPherson began the erection of a fine home at the corner of Maple Street and Maumee Pike. Solomon Gould was the head carpenter and he built the colonial house that is now owned and occupied by the Neil Wagoner family. All the lath and nails were made by hand. The central hall with its walnut staircase separates the two large front rooms, each having a great fireplace. The east parlor opens onto the garden. There is a large room facing Maple Street that they used as dining room and kitchen, with two bedrooms opening from it. Two large rooms upstairs completed what was then the most imposing dwelling in Hamer's Corners. "Gould must have been a very agile man, for, after the raising, he mounted the ridge pole and, swinging a jug of whiskey over his head, cried out, 'This is a very good frame and deserves a good name. Pray, what shall it be?' If there was a name, it is not known."[4]

In the new house, on February 6, 1832, the third child, Russell McPherson, was born; and on August 5, 1835, William, the youngest child, came.

William McPherson sold several lots on both sides of the pike east of Maple Street. Many houses, both log and frame, were built extending almost to the ravine. Directly east of the McPherson home was a long frame house, still standing, that was used as a store and a dwelling. The tavern built by Hamer was on a hill west of Maple Street. Other houses were built on Maple Street, and the Corners began to assume a prosperous appearance.

William (Billy) Hamer and his wife, Kesia Cleveland Hamer, and their young daughter, Jemima, made ready the kind of entertainment needed for their guests, who at first were mainly people in covered wagons going west who stopped for food and rest. Many a settler delighted in visiting the tavern in the evening in order to converse with some traveler from "down east."

CHAPTER III

At School and Play

1. Education at the Corners

The people of the Corners who had been reared in the east, where education was encouraged, demanded that a school be started in their little settlement. It was finally decided to use the log house on the hill opposite the McPherson home for that purpose. Mrs. Lydia Chase, who had taught school in Massachusetts, was engaged to teach. She immediately set about collecting the children whose parents wished them to go to school and who were willing to pay the small fee required for each child.

In the fall of 1832, before James McPherson was four years old, his grandmother took him to school to begin his education. "She was what is now called an old-fashioned teacher and believed in the injunction 'Spare not the rod.' That was part of the system. She wore a wide frilled cap and when she would go for a pupil to give him a 'squitching,' the victim would watch the angle of that cap border, which would determine the degree of punishment. If it lay straight back, look out!"[1]

Facilities for teaching were few indeed. Formal books for reading were lacking until a book-publishing company was established in Cincinnati some time later. Words and sentences were written with charcoal on a board fastened to the wall, and were copied by the children on small boards. Sums were learned the same way. Practically the only book available was the Bible, which was passed around to those not having one and the simplest verses and stories read and learned.

When James was about ten years of age, the Dewey schoolhouse was built. The land it occupied is on Maple Street, about halfway between George and Mulberry streets. It had been donated for school purposes by Judge Dewey, who, with his son-in-law Orrin Woodward, had built and occupied the old "Round House" on Maple at Mulberry. The Dewey schoolhouse was the largest building in the area at that time and was used for meetings of all kinds. Facilities for teaching were much improved.

James loved the hours he spent there reading, improving his penmanship, and learning about the world outside of Hamer's Corners. Russell and Emeline accompanied him to school and they would often pause to look at the brush-choked lane that later became Main Street. Little William, or Billy, as they called him, was usually waiting for them near the lane when school was over.

The children hurried home, for there was always work to be done. James would have to bring in wood for the fireplaces. Russ, who didn't like the work but wished to be with Jimmie, arranged the wood in piles, sometimes suggesting what he thought was an easier way of doing it. Later they would milk the cows together. Emeline would have to prepare the supper if her mother had much weaving or spinning to do. She liked to bake a johnnycake on a board in front of the fire. That, with fresh butter or buttermilk, made a satisfying meal.

Occasionally the boys would find wild honey in the woods for an added treat. In the fall they gathered bushels of walnuts and hickory nuts, which all the family enjoyed in the evening before the blazing fire. Then their grandmother would tell them stories of the Revolution and of the days that followed. Her store of knowledge of the colonial settlers became theirs. They never tired of listening to her and asking questions about "down east." Thus the meager education received at school was augmented by the fireside talks and word pictures from the lips of their teacher-grandmother.

2. Training Day

Training Day in Hamer's Corners was a time of great interest and importance, for it brought together many of the settlers and their families, not only to watch the militia, but to visit friends they seldom saw. Every able-bodied man of voting age in Greencreek Township was required to meet at Hamer's Corners at stated times for military training. Early in the morning of the appointed day, men began to arrive from far and near, on foot or horseback or, if accompanied by the family, in wagons or oxcarts.

> There was not much attempt at military dress, as each man wore his everyday clothes of homespun gray. When a sufficient number of men were assembled, they were formed in line by Colonel Bradley, whose wife was Eliza Guinall. If the rank and file were in motley garb, not so the Colonel, who rode at the head of the column. He was a striking figure, dark-complexioned, with black eyes and hair. He wore a black military coat with brass buttons, and rode a powerful black horse. He also wore a black military hat from which drooped long black ostrich plumes. He was an imposing figure, whose appearance carried great military authority.
>
> The column would form at Guinalls (East Street), march west on the Pike to a prearranged point, then turn about face and march back. Many of the Militia men had no guns, as there was generally but one gun to a family. Those having none used sticks or mullen stalks for drilling, thus acquiring the name "Mullen Stalk Brigade." They marched to the field back of Guinalls where they went through all drills required by law, and fought sham battles. They again paraded down street and then dispersed for dinner.[2]

All this was of absorbing interest to the children of the Corners. When Jimmie McPherson was eleven years of age, he formed all those between seven and eleven years of age into a "Militia" that tried to copy the maneuvers of the elders. The girls wanted to join, and Jimmie allowed them to do so, although Russell doubted that girls would make good soldiers. Jimmie always acted as leader, gave the orders and insisted upon obedience.

The tavern did a thriving business on Training Day, for the men were both hungry and thirsty. At noon the children ran to their homes for a bite to eat and were back again long before the afternoon drill had started. They gathered near Hamer's Tavern and sat or reclined on the ground to watch the men come and go, and to wait for Jemima Hamer, who had to help wait on the guests.

Russell didn't see why it was necessary for him to work so hard that morning. "I would rather not be a soldier, Jimmie," he said.

"Why not?" asked Jimmie.

"Well, it makes me so tired. Can't you kill people without all this drilling and marching?"

"This drilling is not just for the purpose of killing people," said Jimmie. "It is to defend our country and make it strong. A strong army will make people afraid to attack us. You see, Russ, a good strong army will give our country peace."

"Oh! I thought we were just practicing to kill people," replied Russ, who appeared to have lost interest in the work. "I'd rather lay down here and watch those white clouds in the sky."

Jemima came from the tavern and told in an excited manner that she had heard some man talking about runaway slaves he heard were in Amsden's Corners the day before.[3] None of the children had ever seen a Negro. They could not imagine anyone being black all over.

"I'd wash it off if I was black," said Phoebe Russell.

Russ replied, "You couldn't wash it off any more than you can wash off that wart on your nose." That wart was a tender point for Phoebe. She had become aware of it only in the last year and of its fatal effect upon beauty. Hadn't she done everything to banish it? She had faithfully arisen at dawn on the first three mornings of May and washed the wart with May dew, which held great curative powers, she had been told. She thought it was about gone, but with Russell's pointed remark, her consciousness of its presence was almost overwhelming. Jimmie saw her flushed face and said that "he guessed everyone didn't have such sharp eyes as Russ; he hardly noticed anything on her nose," which quickly restored the little girl's happy frame of mind.

Jemima ventured the remark, "Maybe some day a Negro will come on the stage and stop off here at the tavern." That met with expressions of fear, expectation or joy from the children.

Darwin Harkness declared, "My father's a doctor. I think he could do something for the Negroes."

"No," replied Jimmie, "that's something that can't be cured. It's in the blood and skin, and there's really nothing that can change it."

Suggested Russell helpfully, "He could let the blood out."

"That 'ud kill him," shrieked Mary Porter.

"There might be some other way to take off the black," thought Emeline.

Phoebe insinuated, "Russell looks kind of black."

"Some of that can wash off," replied Russ. "Anyway, my blood isn't black."

"Let's cut him and see," said Phoebe's brother John.

Jimmie, trying to steer the conversation away from such bloody thoughts, said, "Father was saying that Nathan Birdseye told him he had seen Negroes in Amsden's Corners. They run away from their masters down south and hide during the day. Then at night someone takes them in a wagon to Portland." The children were more or less awed by this news.

"You mean they stay in Amsden's Corners all day?" asked Jemima.

"That's what he heard," replied Jimmie. "Then at night someone takes them in a load of corn fodder or hay to Portland. Then they ride in a boat to Canada."

"I'll never go to Amsden's Corners with Father again," said Mary.

"You won't see any Negroes there," declared Jimmie. "They hide all day."

"Why do they run away?" asked Phoebe.

"Their masters make them work and whip them if they don't. They don't get any pay for it either. I don't think that's right."

"I wouldn't like that kind of a job," uttered Russell.

That ended the talk, for they saw the men getting in line near the tavern, ready to march to the field again for a short drill. The fifer led on playing "Yankee Doodle" while the men did their best to step up to the spirited music.

At a respectful distance in the rear marched Jimmie McPherson and his "Militia."

3. The Stagecoach

> Shortly after the Western Reserve and Maumee Turnpike were made, the stagecoach made its appearance. There was no scheduled time for its arrival, for, because of the condition of the road, the time might vary considerably. Its coming was an event of great importance, and the children of the Corners would hear the driver's horn in time to run to the top of the hill and station themselves near the Tavern.
>
> They could see the vehicle ploughing its way through the mud, swaying from side to side, coming nearer and nearer. Finally they could see the driver, Tom Shields, gathering up the reins and flourishing the whip for the final plunge up the hill. Then he would bring the horses to a dead stop at the door of the Tavern.[4]

Jimmie McPherson was generally on hand to see if there was any mail. His father was the first postmaster in the township; but if he should be too busy in the smithy or on the farm, he would send one of the boys, preferably Jimmie, to get the mail. Then when he had a little leisure, he would put the few letters in his hat and deliver them.

Jimmie felt the importance of getting and delivering the mail to the postmaster. He also felt that here was a contact with the great world that extended beyond the limits of the Corners; a world represented not only by the mail, but also by the strangers who stopped at the tavern; a world he hoped to see some day.

CHAPTER IV

Friends and Neighbors

William McPherson's closest friends, James Birdseye and his son Nathan, had acquired land in the Ohio country that had been taken partly by purchase and partly as payment for the making of the Western Reserve and Maumee Turnpike. This tract of land consisted of 1800 acres and was located along the turnpike one and a half miles east of Hamer's Corners. The land at the corner of the turnpike and the South Ridge was owned by William Christie, who had come from New York City and had settled first in Lower Sandusky in 1815. He later moved to the newly acquired farm, and built a frame house just south of the turnpike. This house is still in a good state of preservation.

William Christie had two daughters, Abigail, born in 1804, and Mary Ann, born in 1810. Christie, whose brother owned one of the large dry goods stores in New York, was a man of means. He gave his daughters the best education that could be obtained in northern Ohio. Both had been graduated from Norwalk Academy, where they had studied French, English literature and other subjects that were considered advanced west of the Appalachians.

Mary Ann Christie married Nathan Birdseye and they began

their married life in the Christie home. Later they built a large two-story frame house on the corner of the pike and the South Ridge, which location has since been known as Birdseye's Corners. They had one daughter, Cornelia, who was born in 1832.

"Abigail Christie was a dainty, small-boned creature with a round face and blue eyes. When she was in her early twenties, she fell in love with Robert McPherson, brother to Jimmie's father. He loved her in return and they became engaged. Robert was somewhat domineering and Abigail had a will of her own. They argued about many things, particularly about the preparation for their marriage and the disposition of her property. Their marriage day was rapidly approaching, and Abby began wondering if Robert would always insist upon having his own way as he was then doing. She began to resent it and, during an argument, she told him she thought they could not be happy together. That ended their engagement and Robert left for the west. She never saw him again. No one had ever learned how this had affected Abigail. She kept her feelings to herself, but—she never married."[1]

Most of the women and older girls of Hamer's Corners were busy practically all the time. Even when visiting their neighbors they never failed to take along some sewing or knitting; while they talked over recent events or discussed someone's sickness, their fingers constantly plied their work. Any woman who visited without her work brought on her family words of pity because of what they called her "shiftlessness."

Those living on the North Ridge liked to spend a little time with Cynthia McPherson, not only to visit, but also to see the covered wagons passing her door going west—always west. On certain days they had the added pleasure of seeing the stage gathering momentum to climb the hill to the tavern if it were going west, or, if it were going east, they could see Tom Shields pulling on the lines as his "coach and four" came down the hill.

Cynthia McPherson and Mary Ann Birdseye had become fast friends. Mrs. Birdseye would drive the mile and a half to visit Cynthia, bringing her daughter Cornelia and, occasionally,

Abigail. Those were happy occasions for the McPherson children, who loved to have Cornelia come. She, an only child, was four years younger than Jimmie, but, because of her studies in private schools and her visits with her mother and aunt to older people, she seemed older than all the McPherson children except Jimmie, whose natural bearing and actions were those of a cultured youth.

Corneila's great-uncle Christie, who owned the large store in New York, often sent her presents—a bonnet, a piece of jewelry or a book. Nothing had delighted her so much as the book of "Fairy Tales" he had sent her. She had her mother and aunt read the stories to her so often that she knew them word for word, and she would try to enact the scenes that had become real to her.

On her visits to the McPherson home, the children had great fun playing in the grove on pleasant afternoons. The grove was a strip of land extending south of the pike, where now is the Big Four Railroad. There were trees and fallen logs there and a few crude benches. Meetings were sometimes held in the grove in the summer, and it was an ideal place for a playground. Cornelia led the games. She always wanted a fairy play, to which all the others acquiesced with joy. The grove became a castle; Cornelia was the princess, and Jimmie the prince. Russell wanted to be the prince but Cornelia assured him he was not tall enough, so he had better be the ogre or bad fairy.

"What does the ogre do?" asked Russ.

"He tries to carry off the princess," she told him.

Russ thought that would be all right but he didn't think he could lift her. She explained that he could take her by the arm and make her go with him. Then she added, "Then the prince comes on his white horse and rescues the princess."

"Where's the white horse?" asked Russ, thinking this was an impossible play.

"We'll have to make believe. The prince can come partway and leave the horse in the road behind the trees."

Emeline was to be lady in waiting to the princess, and little Billy a page holding a long rod. The prince and princess must have crowns, so grasses and leaves were woven into strands for crowns and necklaces for the principal actors. Jimmie made two wooden swords, one for himself and one for Russ.

When all was ready, Prince James and the ogre left the scene, and Princess Cornelia, with her lady in waiting and her page boy, made preparations for the coming of the prince. Before she was quite ready, the ogre, with drawn sword and his helpers, came stealthily behind the princess, seized her by the arms and were making their getaway in spite of screeches and scratches from the princess and the lady in waiting. They had almost succeeded in their nefarious work when the prince heard the cries of distress, and, in a few agile bounds, he and his servant reached the scene of action.

The ogre turned on the prince and with his sword attempted to stop the rescue. He also tried to bite the serving man, but a few sharp blows from the prince's sword disarmed the ogre, who with his assistant was caught and bound. The princess was then led to the throne by her prince and rescuer.

All the actors declared the play was beautiful, and they never had had such a lovely time.

CHAPTER V

Misfortune

The terrifying panic of 1837 struck like swift lightning on all parts of the country. The "Specie Circular," which instructed land agents to accept no money but gold or silver in payment for public lands, caused many settlers of the new country to lose their farms. President Jackson had practically abolished the United States Bank by distributing its funds to state banks—pet banks as they were called. Jackson thought the state banks safer than the United States Bank, but the result was not what he had expected. Those millions of dollars so close at hand had caused unlooked-for borrowing, investing and speculating, all of which could end in nothing but disaster. When the government saw the results, it demanded "specie payment."

But there was no specie. The people had only paper money. They could not pay their debts, and as a result, many firms became bankrupt and thousands of people lost their homes.

William McPherson, like many of his neighbors, wanted to acquire more land. To this end, he bought a piece now and then when he had enough money for a down payment. He had borrowed money from the bank to pay for the last piece. He sometimes sold some farmland when he could do so at an advantage. All these transactions were settled with paper money and he was slowly forging ahead in the world. He was still paying for his last purchase when the crash came, and he was forced to give it up. This loss caused him much worry and fretfulness. The efforts he had expended in clearing his land, planting and cultivating his fields, combined with his blacksmith trade, had already caused him to be nervous and irritable. His ambition had made him an overworked man, and the new disaster resulted in his being depressed, even moody, at times. This not only increased his nervousness, but resulted in bodily illness that neither doctors nor home remedies could alleviate. His fields had to be let out to strangers and brought him little in return.

His wife, already burdened with the care of her family, tried to raise enough of the staple crops to furnish their necessary food. Emeline had to learn many things about the housework, and had to look after little Billy; she also helped to care for her sick father. James, almost ten years of age, was thoughtful beyond his years. He tried to assume the care of many out-of-door jobs, and helped his mother plant a large field of corn, and hoed it several times during the summer. He milked the cows, cut wood and did other chores difficult for a boy of his age.

Russ, six years of age, was employed to throw stones and clods at the crows that would sometimes descend on the field in flocks. There was an element of fun in that work, for he had a slingshot he used, and he could be near Jimmie. The boys also took care of the sheep. The children didn't consider their work to be unusual, for work was the common lot.

Occasionally there was a rare day when they could roam through the woods to gather wild flowers, to see where the pigeons or eagles made their nests, to look for a bee tree, to gather medicinal herbs or wild strawberries, or sassafras bark to chew, or, in the fall, to gather walnuts or hickory nuts for the winter; there were always Sunday picnics in the summer.

The father's health grew worse steadily for several years until he became an invalid without hope of recovery. As the children grew older it seemed more difficult for Cynthia to provide the things they needed. James and Emeline had to miss school occasionally. In 1840 their grandmother, Mrs. Lydia Chase, who had helped them a great deal in their studies, married Isaac Slocum of Bellevue (formerly Amsden's Corners) and went to that town to live. Cynthia was anxious about her children's education; but she was a woman of prayer and trusted in God for help for her little family.

In March, 1841, before Jimmie was thirteen years old, a friend living near Stemtown learned that Robert Smith, who kept the general store there, needed a boy to help him. The friend suggested Jimmie McPherson to Smith and told him of the boy's fine qualities. Jimmie was delighted when he heard of the prospect of making some money. He could help his mother more than ever. Cynthia, while seeing the help this position would afford them, was reluctant to have Jimmie leave home. Nevertheless, she did not allow her feelings to interfere with what she thought would be best for all the family. Soon everything was arranged for Jimmie to go to Stemtown. Cynthia carefully brushed his mended clothes, braided him a summer hat and, with earnest prayers on his behalf, let him go.

The children, who keenly felt the parting, were warned by their mother to be cheerful when James left home. So they tried to be brave as each one gave him a little gift that he might remember them. It seemed to them he was to be gone forever although he was to visit them every Sunday. Billy, who was six now and going to school, gave him a goose quill he had found in Bosley's yard, telling Jimmie to write to him. Emeline presented him with two pads made from the wool of her favorite sheep. These were to be worn in his shoes so that his thirteen-year-old feet would not get calloused like his father's from standing all day in the store.

Russell almost blubbered when he offered Jimmie his most valued possession—his slingshot. He had made it from an old piece of leather that he had worked over until it was stretchy, and it was considered the best slingshot in Hamer's Corners. However, he said with bravado, "This is a better slingshot than yours and I can make another one."

Jimmie knew what a void the loss of his slingshot would

make in Russell's life, so he said, "That's good of you, brother, but I won't have any time to use it in the store. You keep it and use it on the crows and hawks this summer. I'll give you a penny each week if you kill ten crows before I come home on Sunday."

Russell's dejection lifted noticeably and he began to strut. He said, "I'll have ten crows piled up in the grove every Saturday night." Russell had acquired a business.

A few years later, Jimmie wrote of his first farewell to home: "The whole family were in tears as I kissed them 'Goodby'; taking up my little bundle, I commenced my journey of five miles afoot and alone. After walking boldly for some distance, I looked back and saw them all at the door watching and weeping. To shut out the painful sight I clutched my bundle tighter and ran as fast as my young feet would carry me until I reached the woods, where I sat down and wept abundantly. Then I took up my bundle again and went on to Stemtown."

CHAPTER VI

A Boy's First Position

1. Stemtown

Arriving at the little settlement of Stemtown, James soon found the general store, where he made himself known. Robert Smith took him to the Smith home nearby and introduced James to his wife, Catherine Stem Smith and their little daughter Fannie. Mrs. Smith was attracted to the fine-looking, mannerly lad and at once conceived a motherly feeling for him that persisted all her life. Fannie attached herself to him possessively.

By this time Catherine's young brothers and sisters, Jesse, Leander, Mathias, Clementine, Lydia and Elizabeth Stem, had learned of James's arrival, for the news had spread and they came breathlessly to inspect him. This was an event in the quiet life of the locality. After introductions, all trooped upstairs to the room Catherine had assigned to James. They had to help him arrange his few belongings in the curtained recess back of the door. The rope bed was comfortable and the covers ample. Clemmy said she would bring a picture to place on the wall, and there was a braided rug at home she knew her mother could spare for the room. All these kindly words and gestures warmed the boy's lonely heart.

But he was anxious to get to work. As quickly as possible he went to the store, where Robert began showing him his duties. He must help keep the store clean and orderly; he must learn prices of goods in order to wait on trade; he must help Catherine get wood for the fireplaces, and do other household chores. "He wore a large apron while working and when finished he hung it on a nail behind the door."[1]

He enjoyed working in the store, for in it were all the articles that the settlers of that time could purchase in a small town. He took such pains to please customers that soon it was said that people would come from "as far as Lower Sandusky to have Jimmie McPherson wait on them."

He was attracted by the many books belonging to the Smiths, and when he had time, he was allowed to read what he wished. He pored over Plutarch's *Lives,* Gibbon's *Decline and Fall,* Marshall's *Life of Washington,* Buffon's *Natural History,* and some standard works of fiction. The Smiths encouraged him by discussing with him the book he was reading.

James also liked to draw and had become an artistic penman. When he had time in the store he made little pen and ink sketches, from memory, of the springs and other places of interest on scraps of paper and signed his name to them with many flourishes. He gave some of them to his friends in Stemtown, and brought many to his mother on his weekly trips home. She could give them to whom she pleased, and there were few, if any, in Hamer's Corners who didn't have a sample of Jimmie's artistry.

James began to enjoy life in Stemtown. The Smith's formed a deep liking for him, and their home was his second home. Robert Smith was a man of many interests. "He owned five big farms and several grist- and sawmills. His father-in-law, Jacob Stem, was a moneyed man who had come early from Maryland and bought all the land occupied by Stemtown and surroundings. He employed tutors for his family of ten children. He bought them the first melodeon in that locality, because of his love for music. Both he and Robert Smith made occasional business trips to New York and always brought back several pieces of music or some songbooks. The children pounced upon them eagerly and soon the Stem home resounded to the new melodies."[2]

Clemmy Stem, who was three years younger than Jimmie, showed her liking for him by many little acts of kindness; she would help him in the store when she could, and often made him some little gift. She always stood near him when the children sang together around the melodeon. Jimmie was grateful for these little attentions, and he regarded all the Stem children as near brothers and sisters. One of their favorite songs was the first published work of Stephen Collins Foster, "Open Thy Lattice, Love." They formed a liking for the songs of this composer, and looked forward to his new ones. Thus in the little settlements of the north Ohio woods were sung the melodies that were being heard in the cities of the east. New York was brought to Stemtown; also to Cornelia at Birdseye's Corners. Jimmie and Cornelia brought the songs to Hamer's Corners, where they and their young friends loved to talk about these worldly subjects after having attended Sunday school in the Dewey schoolhouse.

This worldliness which was invading Hamer's Corners was regarded with distaste by some of their neighbors who looked upon these goings-on as little short of wickedness. In fact, it appeared to some that Satan was coming a little too close to their town. The Birdseyes and the McPhersons belonged to the Universalist Church at that time; but there were people of that persuasion, also the Methodists, "who frowned upon secular music as an evil thing, and dancing as the work of the devil. A violin, especially if it had ever been played for dancing, was to be despised; and a hall or room that had once witnessed young people in the quadrille or polka was to be shunned, it being deemed a sin even to glance in its direction."[3]

These forbidden subjects were often discussed by the young people after church services on Sunday, which was almost the only time during the week that they could be together. While the older people talked outside the Dewey school, the McPherson children and Cornelia, the young Russells, Jemima Hamer, Darwin Harkness, the Porters, Guinalls and others walked slowly toward the McPherson home, which had become a meeting place for them. This walk after church was looked forward to as the pleasantest time of the week.

Cornelia, who was attending private school in Lower Sandusky, and who, in spite of her tender years, was more worldly wise than the other children, couldn't see why anything that gave one so much pleasure as music and dancing should be forbidden. She said, "I have the loveliest thoughts when I sing and when I dance, too."

"You don't really dance, do you, Cornelia?" said Phoebe Russell. "You'll surely go to hell for it."

Cornelia executed a few steps to the horror of Phoebe and Mary Porter, who spread out their wide skirts and tried to hide her from anyone who might be looking.

Jemima said she thought she would like to dance. More horror! Jimmie thought the Bible didn't say anything against it. Russell added that he would like to take a peek in Bosley's hall, where dances were sometimes held.

"Do you want to go to hell?" asked Mary.

"I wouldn't if you were there," answered Russ.

"Well, I'm not going there," snapped Mary.

Russell said, "It might not be so bad to look at. I'd like to travel and see places." His idea of hell was somewhat obscure.

Jimmie said, "You'll have to work if you go there."

"Work! Guess I won't go then."

Jimmie remarked thoughtfully, "Dancing seems to make people happy. Don't you think it is all right to be happy?"

Phoebe replied, "It's all right if you're good. But just the same we shouldn't look into that dance hall."

"How am I ever going to know how bad it is if I don't look?" asked Russell.

Said Emeline, glad for a chance to change the conversation, "Here we are at home. Couldn't we try some of the songs Jimmie brought from Stemtown?"

They went eagerly into the house and were soon singing without accompaniment, although Phoebe and Mary weren't quite sure that it was not a sinful act.

Two neighbors, Mrs. Nancy Rowen and Mrs. Lydia Craxton,

were walking home from meeting a little behind the young people, trying to hear what they said; they were also discussing many of the things they had seen and heard that morning. The subject drawing their first attention was the spiritualist meeting that had been held the previous week in Henry Brown's house. A woman who called herself a medium claimed she had talked with spirits.

"Spirits!" exclaimed Nancy. "You mean in a jug?"

"No," replied Lydia, "I mean the dead come to life." Nancy's big eyes rolled in their sockets. "Spirits of the dead," Lydia continued. "She talked with William Hogsden and Oliver Smith, and land knows, they've been spirits four years come fall. Ames said he heard the spirits knocking."

Nancy looked frightened as she said, "I'm afraid that Satan is coming to the Corners!" They had reached the McPherson home and heard the young voices singing.

"You say he's coming?" exclaimed Lydia. "Listen! He's here now. What do you think of that?" They stopped a moment. "It's no wonder William is a sick man; it's no wonder, the way the young people are carrying on. None of us are safe."

Nancy looked around fearfully as if expecting the "Old Boy" near and ready to snatch her away any minute. She said, "We'd better be hurrying home," starting as if to go and looking around for Lydia to follow. But Lydia wanted to see as well as to hear. She moved toward the open door and, to her horror, saw Cornelia, with hands holding skirts, taking some dance steps across the floor as the others sang. Jimmie saw Lydia and came to the door to invite her in; but her curiosity was sated; she said she just wanted to ask about his father. She left immediately to retail the awful scene to Nancy.

2. Stemtown Friends

Besides the young people in the Stem and Smith families, there were the Dawley boys and Elijah Brownell, living near Stemtown, who had become particular friends of James. He also had become acquainted with young Rutherford B. Hayes, who had just opened a law office in Lower Sandusky. Hayes had become acquainted with the Stem family and made frequent calls there. He seemed to admire Elizabeth Stem.

"In a letter to his sister, Mrs. W. A. Platt, written from Lower Sandusky, April 20, 1845, he said: 'I've been to Stemtown with Uncle and like the family well. I did not see her.' "

In another letter, written in 1847, he wrote: "My dear Fanny, I spent a Sunday a fortnight ago at Stemtown with the girls and Miss Gardener of Columbus."[4]

"One day in September, 1848, James, with Elijah, or 'Lige' as they called him, the Dawley boys and Rutherford Hayes, went hunting in the Stem woods. With James ahead and Lige following, each spied a squirrel at the same moment and each aimed and fired. There was the report of one gun and the squirrel fell. Each claimed the squirrel. Lige, said, 'Look at your gun, Jimmie.' James looked and was amazed that his gun had not been fired.' He had had few opportunities to use a gun, never having owned one. Lige thought James excitable, no doubt because his mind worked and formed judgments so quickly as to give that impression. But in this case, the squirrel had made his heart beat rapidly. He said to Lige, 'I'll get the next one.'

"Lige had a sister, Berintha, two years younger than Jimmie. She was a very pretty girl. Jimmie frequently walked to the Brownell home on the Lower Sandusky road to see her. There is no record that this was anything more than a boy and girl affair which ended when Jimmie went away to school."[5]

CHAPTER VII

Norwalk Academy

New York papers that came to the Smith home carried stories about the great number of Americans who had entered the vast territory called Texas, and had acquired immense tracts of land. Texas was annexed in 1845; in 1846 the Mexicans attacked the Americans on the north side of the Rio Grande.

News of these happenings came regularly to Stemtown via the New York papers. James pored over their contents and discussed them with Robert and Catherine. He was approaching his eighteenth year and had given some thought to plans for his life's work. He could settle on nothing definitely, for he felt there was little opportunity for him in Stemtown or Hamer's Corners. The exciting events described in the papers fired his imagination and aroused in him a desire to take part in them.

He was now a young man with strength and vitality and a determination to make something of himself if it were possible. Adventure in Texas appealed to him. There, it seemed to him, lay his chance to make a fortune. Through his constant reading and studying by late candlelight, he had acquired a better education than the pioneers and their children of the area possessed. He could use his knowledge to good advantage in the great country to the southwest.

But Robert Smith had different ideas for his young helper and protégé. He had grown fond of James and disliked the thought of his going so far from home. He and James discussed the subject many times. He encouraged the boy to continue his studies in Stemtown for a year, then take a term or two of formal education in Norwalk Academy. Robert would help to defray expenses. If James could pass the necessary examination for the Military Academy at West Point, Robert said, he would get Rudolphus Dickinson, then Congressman from the Tiffin district, to appoint him to that coveted place.

That, indeed, was a prize to strive for; adventure in Texas paled before it. James doubled his efforts at self-education. "Jacob Stem said he would allow the tutors he employed for his children to give him some time each week in order to guide him in the studies he needed."[1]

Great was the joy in the McPherson home when James told his family he might get into West Point Academy. Cynthia determined in her mind that she would give him all the help she could. The happy news served to lift her from the depression into which her husband's increasing illness had plunged her.

William was steadily growing more nervous and harder to care for. Then, a great weakness, which was probably pernicious anemia, sapped all his desire to get well. Doctors Harkness and Seeley agreed he was beyond their help. But Cynthia, with that great hope and resourcefulness so characteristic of her, gathered herbs known to be healing and made infusions for him. She made appetizing drinks of whey to which she added wild honey, or hop tea and other simple home remedies. But nothing helped him. He gradually sank into a condition in which he lay for some time, not recognizing his beloved wife and children. On September 16, 1847, he passed away.

In the fall of 1848 James McPherson entered Norwalk Academy. Thus began a new and exciting era of his life. Robert Smith drove him to the town twenty miles east of Hamer's Corners, the greatest distance from home that James had traveled as yet. He was, indeed, going out into the world. Even those settlers who had come from "York State" thought it a "powerful ways off to go to get larnin'" Emeline, Russ and Billy could form little conception of the distance. They only knew he would be gone a long time.

Cynthia had spent much time weaving, coloring and making his clothes. Robert had given him several items of clothing, including a round felt hat and some cravats. James was now almost six feet tall, slim and graceful in his movements; and when he was arrayed in his new clothes, he presented a picture that Cynthia could have gazed at forever. Instead, she saw to it that the small bag of clothing he was taking was secure, and that his box of precious books loaned him by Robert had a place of safety. When all was ready he kissed his dear ones good-by, promising them to write occasionally. He jumped into the carriage with Robert, who started the horses at once.

Several of their friends and neighbors had joined the McPhersons in gazing at the unusual spectacle—a young man from the Corners going off to school in a carriage. All wished him good-by and Godspeed.

Norwalk Academy was the largest and most famous institution of its kind west of the Alleghenies at that time.

> A large brick building three stories in height is devoted to its purposes. It is flourishing and numbers over 100 pupils, including both sexes. Charles H. Stewart, Esq. in an address delivered March 27, 1883, at the farewell reunion of the Academy Alumni, said, "Everybody kept boarders; in fact, that was about the main occupation of about nine-tenths of our able-bodied citizens during that period. Board was very reasonable. A young man could get the best room and finest board in town for from $1.00 to $1.50 per week. Mutton sold for 2¢ a pound; and as everybody kept cows and pigs and hens which all ran free in the street, milk, pork and eggs were almost given away. Our late President R. B. Hayes, our present Governor Charles Foster, the late General James B. McPherson and several of our Congressmen were dormitory boys who cooked and ate

and devised mischief there. The boys had their bread baked there, did the rest of their cooking, and lived nicely for 40¢ a week including room rent which was $1.00 a term."

C. E. Newman, librarian of the Firelands Historical Society (1886), told Mr. Howe: "The people of Norwalk have a natural pride in the fact that General James B. McPherson was once a student in their old Academy. He boarded with me. He was a very studious, gentlemanly youth with the highest reputation for capacity."

He narrowly escaped failing to get into the Military Academy. He had applied for and was expecting the appointment when Rudolphus Dickinson, the member of Congress through whom it was to come, suddenly sickened and died. McPherson was then in an agony of suspense. No one could give him any information whether the cadet warrant for admission into the Academy had been granted. At the last moment the warrant was found among Dickinson's papers. As it was, James had to hurry, and he narrowly escaped getting to West Point in time.[2]

CHAPTER VIII

West Point

The McPherson home was the scene of great activity on that May day in 1849 when James was to leave for West Point. Robert Smith had gone to Lower Sandusky when he heard of the Congressman's death, and it was his insistence that Dickinson's papers be examined at once that resulted in the appointment paper being found in time for the examination. He sped to Hamer's Corners on horseback to give the paper to James. Excitement and happiness reigned as all rushed to help James get ready for the trip.

Russell was to accompany him to Sandusky, where he was to take the boat to Buffalo. They were no sooner ready and out on the pike when the stage came from the tavern. The carpetbag was put on top of the stage, and Tom Shields, the driver, let the young men sit with him. Then with a great flourish of his whip they were off. At Bellevue they took a train on the Sandusky and Mad River Railroad to Sandusky. It was their first ride on the cars and it furnished them with all the thrills they had anticipated. The locomotive puffed and shuddered to attain the amazing speed of twelve miles an hour. Several times the train stopped at stated places to put on wood and water.

At Sandusky they had a few hours to wait before the boat left, so they walked around the town for a while. They were impressed by the buildings made of stone, and they were interested in the "Porter House" facing the bay, where Charles Dickens had stayed in 1842 while on his "American Tour."

But they were anxious to get into the *Baltic* and see the arrangement of things. All too soon the signal for departure came and Russell bade James good-by and left the boat. He stood on the wharf for some time watching the vessel until it disappeared around the point of land known as Cedar Point. His imagination was inflamed with the thought of the new life opening for James. Surely there would be adventure in it as well as education. Above all James would see the world. Russ made up his mind that he, too, would acquire an education. He was doing well managing the store and he would be able to save money. His mind was full of the subject on his return trip to Hamer's Corners.

When James saw the shore and Russell receding from his view he had a momentary feeling of loss. But as the boat rounded the wooded point of land and struck out further from shore, he looked around at the vast expanse of water. A sense of beauty and then a smell of adventure created in him a delightful emotion. He sensed that beyond the dim horizon to which the swaying boat was carrying him lay his future life. His eyes could not penetrate the hazy curtain resting on the water; he wished the boat would hasten, for he wanted to see what lay beyond.

In due time he arrived at Buffalo, where he met a young man from Arkansas by the name of Rector who had been at West Point the previous year. As they traveled together, the cadet gave James a resumé of the rules and customs of the school. He described the buildings and grounds so accurately that James felt almost at home when he arrived there. He lost the notion he had that he would appear "green" to the other fellows. That put him at his ease and he entered into all the preliminaries attendant upon his entry with zest.

In his first letter to Russ, dated July 12, 1849 he told of some of the regulations and the drills which he did not enjoy at first. At the parades he had to stand perfectly erect and motionless for half an hour with his eyes directly to the front while there was the strongest inducement to turn them to one side, for the old cadets were parading and the band was playing some splendid tunes. After a couple of weeks he got used to it and he began to enjoy himself. He was examined on the second day of June and on the same day went into camp. He said, "I went on guard Friday for the first time. I had to walk post 8 hours out of the 24–2 hours on and 4 hours off. Monday I commenced artillery drill, which I like very much.

"When the new Cadets first came, the old Cadets were much disposed to run it on us—called us Plebes—and would come around and try to make us believe they were Corporals and had authority to order us every night and make us perform some extra duty. But they have almost given that up, for some of them got caught at it and were severely punished."

James wrote frequently to Russell encouraging him to go to school. Although the latter was studiously inclined, he wished to get a good education mainly because, by doing so, he would continue to be close to James. The letters coming to him from West Point showed him that James was living in a different world from his own. But the military life did not interest Russell. It was the realm of learning and of books that appealed to him and that gave him a great desire to live with James in that enchanted region.

In October, 1849, James wrote him of the fine sport they were having in the skirmish drills, such as getting behind trees and rocks in order to be secure while firing at an enemy; going through the operation of loading and firing and running at top speed with fixed bayonets.

May was the time for selecting corporals and they were chosen from those who had been there one year. James thought it amusing to see how military the cadets had become who had just emerged from their "plebeianship," and who coveted the promotion. He was one of those so elevated. The corporals increased, when possible, their military appearance on May 11, 1850. On that day General Winfield Scott visited the academy. A salute of fifteen guns was fired from the cadet battery in his honor. Although sixty-seven years of age, he was of majestic appearance, and his step was firm and elastic. The cadets entertained great respect for him, because his influence had always been exerted in their behalf.

In June, James wrote his ma for a few dollars, if she could send it, as he would have no money until furlough. He wished to return treats to his friends. He received five dollars in reply and wrote: "Thanks is the only means I have of repaying you now. I have tried to get along as cheaply as possible, and on the first of the month was $9 in debt. But during this year I'll not have to purchase as many things as last, so I think I can save something."

James writes to Russ from Camp Gaines, West Point, on July 30, 1850: "This is party night and the fellows are just fixing to go. The ladies who attend are mostly visitors who are spending a few weeks here, and some of them are perfect beauties. Perhaps I ought not to have added the word perfect, but you must make all due allowance, for when a fellow has been deprived of the society of ladies for 10 months they appear unusually interesting.

"Yesterday after artillery drill, we had a treat of cakes and whortleberries sent into the camp for the Cadets by Mrs. Gen. Scott—over a bushel of cakes and a half bushel of berries."

The parties that formed a diversion for the cadets were planned seriously by them in order to entertain their lady friends who visited them. Dancing was the number one amusement. James enjoyed it and was now a graceful dancer. One song that met with popular acclaim at that time was Foster's "Oh, Susannah," and it was sung and danced to with much enthusiasm. Fortunately, the cadets were young enough not to be too deeply affected by the disputes brought on by the slavery question, which had been settled for the time being by the Compromise of 1850. Those disputes between northern and southern factions appeared to them mere political fracases. They enjoyed their parties and other social functions, and in every way led a busy, normal life.

James wrote to Russell on April 5, 1851, telling him how gratified he was to learn he was attending Norwalk Academy.

He informed Russ that Miss Stewart and Miss Otis were attending there, also; he asked Russ to give them his best respects if he had become acquainted with them. If Russell had become acquainted with the young ladies, it was no fault of his, for he generally kept his distance when they appeared upon the scene. But since James had made the request, Russell would comply with it regardless of his somewhat unsocial manner, or of its effect upon himself. James would always be served by Russell.

In a letter to Clemmy Stem, April 22, 1851, at the Conservatory of Music in Cincinnati, James wrote:[1]

> Ever since I heard you had arrived in Cincinnati I have been anxious to know how you have been enjoying yourself. I wish you could be here to enjoy the view from my window. You would be delighted. Immediately in front is the plain on which we drill, covered with a green carpet. Beyond is the broad surface of the Hudson glittering in the setting sun and dotted here and there with many sailing vessels. Far in the distance are the Catskill Mountains tinged with golden hues against the blue sky.
>
> I suppose you had the pleasure of hearing Jenny Lind before now. Write and tell me what you think of her.

In August, 1851, James had a two weeks' vacation, which he spent with his mother. There were social affairs arranged for him by Cornelia Birdseye, and the Smiths in Greensprings.

> When James was home, the Sunday schools of the county arranged a big picnic to be held in Greensprings. A prize was offered to the school making the best appearance in the parade. McPherson became interested and made a banner on which he painted a beautiful picture and presented it to the Clyde school to be used in the parade.
>
> The picture was of a lion and a lamb lying peacefully together with a little child standing by holding them

with a cord. At the bottom of the picture was the quotation from the Bible,

"The lion and the lamb shall lie down together and a little child shall lead them."

This picture won the coveted prize for the Clyde school.[2]

James returned to West Point by way of Sandusky and Buffalo. In the latter city he met two cadets returning to the point. They took the cars to New York City, traveling, as James said, "a little less than greased lightning" (fifteen miles an hour). In New York he spent four days visiting the Theater Museum, the Navy Yard and other places of interest.

James wrote home on November 21, 1851, to tell the folks he was studying mechanics, chemistry and drawing, which he practiced two hours a day. He said:

> I have fine times now at riding, as we have commenced to make our horses gallop, jump over poles, etc. It is exciting to be one of sixty to go charging over the plain with sabres drawn and horses at full run. But the richest scene is when some fellow's horse gets the advantage of him a little and breaks out of the platoon and starts for the stables. If the rider closes his legs in order to stop the horse it only sticks the spurs into the horse, making him go faster than ever.

James communicated to Russell in Ann Arbor, January 7, 1852:

> I've been busy preparing for the semi-annual examination which commenced last Friday. Yesterday I assisted in putting up the drawings so that they might be examined in order to make out the standing. Will commence painting after examination.
>
> I don't see how you can resist the charms of such a trio of ladies as you have described in your last. You must be on the alert or they will attack you in some vulnerable spot. You never knew what a narrow escape

I had from a "Wolverine" girl just before coming here. I'll stop! Enough nonsense for this time.

All nonsense to the contrary, James and his friends prepared for the dances painstakingly when they were to meet the ladies. In March, 1852, he describes some of the preparations:

> In order to get in trim for encampment, the members of my class are meeting three evenings a week for a "Stag Dance." To make up for the sad lack of girls, some of us tie a white handkerchief around our necks and gracefully move through the "Mystic Dance" to the sound of the violin played by the "Old Bugler" who is always on hand when we want him. Just imagine your brother Jim enacting the part of a lady and moving with that air of grace with which he is noted, and you must form a pretty correct idea of what our dance must be.
>
> I'm getting so I can dance the Polka, Polka Redown, Hop waltz, Schottische, and the Lord only knows what else.
>
> I received the school catalogue you sent me and I was pleased to see your name among those who are going to take a regular course.

In May, 1852, James learned from Emeline that the name Hamer's Corners no longer existed. Letters sent there in the past had been addressed not only to Hamer's Corners but also to Greencreek and Centerville. But now two railroads, the Cleveland and Toledo and the Sandusky and Tiffin, were being built through the town, forming a junction. This gave an impetus to its growth and a new name for it was demanded. "We are no longer a Corners," people said, and the renaming of the town became a serious community affair.

At a meeting held in Whicher's Tavern (formerly Hamer's) the name "Clyde" was chosen because some of those attending and voting came from Clyde, New York. Several of the latter were strangers who had got off the stagecoach an hour previous to the meeting.

Emeline enclosed ten dollars, "Ma says she may be able to send you more."

James told his family, June 11, 1852, that since the first of June he had been hearing a section of the candidates in arithmetic, and had been excused from all military duty. "It is luxurious," he said, "when reveille beats at five in the morning and my roommates are hustling around so as to get down in time to answer to their names, to wake up just enough to feel conscious that I do not have to get up, and then turn over and take a comfortable snooze until the drum beats for breakfast."

CHAPTER IX

On Furlough From West Point

In the summer of 1852 Cadet James B. McPherson was home two weeks on furlough. His friends in Clyde and vicinity tried to show the tall, handsome youth the honor they thought fitting to extend to a student of the United States Military Academy. His fine figure clothed in the attractive and, to many, the romantic uniform of a cadet drew much attention. He came by way of Buffalo, by boat to Sandusky, then by the Mad River Railroad to Bellevue, where he was met by his brothers Russell and Billy, who proudly drove him home in the light wagon.

Russell wanted Billy to drive, as that gave him an opportunity to converse with Jimmie without the mental effort he required for driving. He had prepared several statements for Jimmie's ear which he had clothed in what he thought was "educated language." He wished to impress his brother with the culture he had received at Norwalk Academy. Perhaps it was the joy he felt at sitting beside his elder brother again; maybe it was the fine clothes that Jimmie wore; something caused the usually talkative Russ to forget the big words he enjoyed using. Finally he said with a solemn look on his round face, "Is the Mad River Road still mad?"

Jimmie laughed and replied, "It must have been a little that way, since it jerked us around considerably."

Billy broke in, "I think Russ is the one that is mad for not getting a ride on the cars."

"They're building a railroad through Clyde this summer," said Russ.

Jimmie thought that would make a great change, and added, "It's amazing the changes the railroads are making in the east, isn't it?"

Billy informed James they had stopped at the Birdseyes on the way to Bellevue. "Cornelia wants you to call."

They made a stop there and were met by Cornelia and her mother. "Welcome home, Cousin," said Cornelia, laughing happily. They went into the large sitting room, where they talked for a time, and then into the parlor around the piano, where they had a session of singing their favorite songs.

Cornelia told James of a party that the elder Miss Latimore of Bellevue was giving the next Thursday afternoon.

"She's invited you, Jimmie. You can get a horse from Henry Niles." He planned to call for her.

Soon the boys were riding the mile and a half home. Needless to say, Jimmie's reception by his mother and sister was all that could be expected. Hungry eyes feasted on him, and longing ears caught every intonation as he told them of his year's work and study, interspersed with many pleasant incidents. He regaled them with stories of some of his classmates and others with whom he had become more than friendly; of his roommate, John Hood, who would much rather give his evenings to fun than to study, and who, next day, would surreptitiously ask Jimmie to help him with his answers; of John Schofield, brilliant in his studies but plentiful in demerits; of Phil Sheridan, an Ohio boy, whose work was mediocre but whose cavalry practice was notable; of George Washington Custis Lee, son of Colonel Robert E. Lee, and great-grandson of Martha Custis Washington, who told Jimmie stories about Arlington, his home on the Potomac; and of many other cadet friends. All visible things ceased to exist for them as he carried them here and there on the campus or the drill ground, to Fort Put or the eagle's nest, to the Hudson or on the cars to New York City.

The next day Jimmie walked to Greensprings to visit his beloved friends and benefactors, Robert Smith and family and the Stems. It was four years since he had left them to enter Norwalk Academy. He tried to go into the Smith home by way of the kitchen, but they saw him coming and all rushed out to meet him. When they entered the spacious house, Jimmie went directly to the kitchen to see if the work apron he used to wear was still behind the door. "It's still here!" he exclaimed.

"Yes," he was told, "we intend to keep it there."[1]

He must know everything about the springs; so they related events that had transpired since he was last there. Catherine said her father, Jacob Stem, was not well; Lucius had just got married; Stemtown was really growing now that a railroad was coming through; some doctors had taken water from the springs to Cleveland for examination.

Clemmy was overseeing preparations for dinner and didn't say much, but her pleasure was noticeable. The hired girl stopped now and then to listen to the conversation, but Clemmy saw to it that she didn't stop long.

When Robert came in, he threw his arms around James. "My boy!" he exclaimed. The eyes of both were bright with tears.

Soon came the call to dinner. The mahogany table was spread to its full length in the long dining room, and the whole family, together with as many of Robert's and Catherine's brothers and sisters as they could summon, sat down to the sumptuous feast. Jimmie was urged to tell about West Point, and he related many of the tales he had told the previous evening at home.

Late in the afternoon he had to leave for Clyde, and Clemmy walked with him past the springs. She was attractive in a dress of white lawn with small pink roses, and her rose-trimmed bonnet looked well with her rosy cheeks, black eyes and black hair drawn smoothly to the curls over her ears. She had had so much to say to Jimmie and she had imagined several conversations she would have with him when he was with her. But now that he was walking beside her, a feeling of near panic seized her and she was almost silent. She could not understand herself.

"You're looking lovely today, Clemmy," Jimmie said at length.

Clemmy was aware that her large Roman nose detracted from an otherwise lovely face. The knowledge made her a little self-conscious.

She replied, "Do you think so? I suppose it must be my new bonnet."

"Not altogether," he said and they both laughed. They had reached the spring and stood looking at the fountain of greenish water rising two feet high, then falling over green and white stones and gliding into a little stream. For years people had come there to drink the water and to carry it home. "It is medicine," they said. Robert Smith was planning to form a company to build a sanitarium where people could come and stay a few days to drink the water.

"This will be a great place some day," said Jimmie. Clemmy was sorry he had changed the subject and wondered, "Just what does he think of me?"

"We hope it will," replied Clemmy. "Then maybe we can have some neighbors of our class."

Jimmie asked about her music and her study in Cincinnati. "Yes, Jennie Lind was all that the papers had said of her and more." They cleared up several matters they had written about. But Jimmie did not say the words she had been looking for; the words she had been hoping to hear.

He at last told her that his mother was having his Uncle Norton's and Uncle William's families for supper that evening and was expecting him home, and he didn't want to keep them waiting. He bade her good-by and said he would see her again before leaving for West Point.

Next morning the boys got up early, Billy to milk the cows, and Jimmie and Russ to witness the operation. Jimmie noted the changes that had been made and the trees that had been cut. "To grow more beans," said Russ. Jimmie also wanted to talk to Billy about his education. Billy, sixteen years of age, didn't think he needed any more education for farming. "I'll have to grub out acres of stumps, and plant wheat and corn. How will French and algebra help me with that?"

"They will help you to become a country gentleman," said Russ.

"Then I'll be the only one around here and that would make me lonesome," replied Billy.

Daisy the cow appeared to resent the presence of her milker's brothers, and began to thrash and kick. Billy tried to quiet her, saying roughly, "So, boss."

Russ said, "If you'd use polite language to her, she'd do better."

Billy sniffed. "She's not used to it and she wouldn't understand it."

"Let me try to quiet her," said Russ. Going up to her, he murmured, "My lady, please observe the proprieties."

The cow swished her tail savagely. The boys laughed.

"Excuse me, gentlemen," Russ insisted, "I omitted something." Turning to Daisy, he said in a voice dripping with sweetness, "My *young* lady, I beg of you to desist. Please observe the proprieties and subside."

Daisy eyed him for a moment. The honeyed words may have had their effect upon her, for she subsided at once.

"You see, Billy, how useful educated language could be in your profession."

At last Thursday came and Jimmie made ready for the party in Bellevue. He had engaged a riding horse from Henry Niles and before dinner was in the saddle. He cantered along the rolling turnpike, noting the changes that the year had brought. Many new fields had been cleared and were under cultivation. Occasionally there was a new frame house. Much virgin forest remained, and giant oaks and walnuts were laced together with wild-grape vines. Locust trees were white with blossoms, and bittersweet with shining leaves clambered over shrubs and rail fences. The warm summer sun glistened on leaves; pools of water beside the road caught the glory of sky, clouds and trees.

Jimmie reached the Birdseye home in time for the noonday meal. He and Cornelia then prepared for the ride to Bellevue.

Cornelia's party gown was carried in a large saddlebag. She was dressed in a riding habit made of green poplin, with a short jacket, and a brown bonnet with a green plume. Jimmie helped her mount and arranged the flowing skirt that reached almost to the ground.

They started the horses, waved to the household, and were off at a fair speed. The picture of the riders caused many a native to stop and stare in amazement and pleasure.

Arriving at the Latimore home on East Main Street, Cornelia engaged the services of Tessie, a younger sister of Miss Latimore, to help her dress for the party. She had to borrow the hoop skirts; she could not wear them riding, neither could she pack them in the saddlebag. Her dress was a delicate shade of green lawn, the voluminous skirt being trimmed with many ruffles. Her brown hair was smoothed down to her ears, then fell in many ringlets almost to her white shoulders.

When she entered the drawing room Jimmie immediately went to her side. The gay young crowd were now entering into the always fun-provoking game of "blindman's buff," which was followed by "thimble, thimble." Out on the lawn, croquet was played by some, while the more active young people seemed to prefer the exciting "drop the handkerchief."

While Jimmie was Cornelia's partner many times, another young man by the name of Isaac Amsden showed a deep interest in her. His people were the first to settle in Bellevue, which was then called Amsden's Corners. He had known Cornelia for some time, having met her at previous social affairs. She tried to divide her time between Jimmie and Isaac.

By the time the delicious supper had been consumed, the sun was reaching down toward the tops of the forest trees, and the guests made ready to leave. "Let's take Jimmie and Neelie a piece," said one. That suited all except possibly Jimmie, and with one accord they turned west on the pike, with Jimmie leading his horse and Isaac leading Cornelia's.

As they approached the county line road they noticed three men on horseback in front of Ed Miller's livery barn.[2] One of the men jumped down and approached Miller, who was standing in front of the barn. The horses were breathing hard and evidently had been driven at top speed. The man's companions joined him and engaged Miller in conversation. As the young group passed the barn the talking became louder and they could hear the words "darkies, runaways."

This frightened the girls, who backed away. The boys, scenting adventure, stood near. This discomfited the first horseman, who looked around at the crowd and displayed a dark face that would have been handsome but for the hard expression on it.

He said, "This is not your affair. I am looking for some of my property that I think is here."

Jimmie, who well knew the man's meaning, replied politely, "You think this man has some of your horses?"

This seemed to enrage the young man, who swore and shouted, "I didn't come all the way from Kentucky to get any horses. We've got better horses in Kentucky than you can find anywhere in this damned state."

Jimmie said firmly, "We don't care what you're looking for but you'd better leave your swearing back in Kentucky."

"Mr. Piety Boy!" was the sarcastic answer, at which his two companions snickered.

Miller addressed the boys, "He thinks there are some of his runaways around here. I guess nobody ever seen any," he lied affably. "No, siree. Did you boys ever see any?"

"No," they shouted.

The leader produced a warrant, written in Columbus, he claimed, allowing him to search any premises that might harbor runaways.

Miller exclaimed, "That's no proof that you have any right and I'll be damned if anyone I don't know is going to search any of my property." The three men proceeded to walk toward the barn.

Jimmie told the boys, "We'll have to interfere here. Come on, boys, let's rush this," and started toward the barn. All the boys followed Jimmie's stalwart figure, and the three men were turned around quickly and pushed toward their horses. Jimmie had the leader by the arms and held him in such a vise that he was helpless. When Jimmie loosened his hold the enraged man turned and deliberately spat on Jimmie's coat. "See how they'll like that at West Point," he sneered. Jimmie was so beside himself at this insult to his uniform that he hit the man with all his force and knocked him down.

"Make him salute that uniform," shouted one of the boys. The others took up the cry. They pulled him to his feet and compelled him to salute the West Point uniform. They threatened violence if he didn't. So, in a cringing manner, he made several attempts until they were finally satisfied with his salute. As he got on his horse he turned to Jimmie and snarled, "I'll get even with you for this." Then the three dashed off toward the Columbus Pike.

Some of the boys took out their handkerchiefs and proceeded to clean the desecrated spot on the uniform. Miller told them there was a good-looking Negro woman nearby that he thought the man was after. He thanked the boys for their help.

After the fright and excitement had subsided, Jimmie and Cornelia bade the group good night and began their ride home. The sun had gone below the treetops but the gold of its setting could be seen ahead. It was spilling a golden haze through the trees and onto the road before them. They didn't say much as they cantered along; their thoughts were of the exciting events in which they had just participated.

When they had come within a mile of Birdseye's Corners, they heard the shrill whistle of the locomotive on the new railroad that paralleled the pike a short distance to the south. The locomotive was going west.

Cornelia exclaimed, "Jimmie, wouldn't it be fun to race the locomotive?"

Jimmie agreed and they put their horses to a gallop. The locomotive could be seen through the trees belching forth smoke and flame. The three travelers ran nip and tuck the entire mile and all three arrived at the South Ridge at the same moment.

Cornelia's bonnet was flying behind her with its ties almost choking her, and her hair was disheveled as they came to a stop in the Birdseye driveway. Jimmie could see her excited, girlish face, happy with the new thrilling experience. As he helped her down she said, "Wasn't that fun?" He held her a little longer than necessary. "I enjoyed it, Cornelia," he answered.

Cornelia went on, "What will Mother say? You know she has always said I am wild. You must help me smooth my hair. Where is my bonnet?" And with such remarks they managed to bring back her pretty, dignified air.

He took her hands in his and said, "I thought you were grown-up but I see you are still the same little girl I have always known. I hope you will never change. I think of you so much, Cornelia, but I am not in a position now to tell you how I feel. But I want you to know you will always be first in my thoughts."

Soon he bade her good night and started for home.

After Jimmie had left her, Cornelia was quieter than usual and retired to her room early. Suddenly she decided she wanted to talk to her Aunt Abby. Crossing the hall, she knocked and, at a gentle "Come in," entered her aunt's room. Abby was writing the simple record of her life as she had daily for years. She welcomed her dear niece with pleasure. They often had talks together on seemingly grave problems that entered Cornelia's life, and the latter always enjoyed the sage remarks and advice of her aunt.

"I think, Aunt Abby," Cornelia said at length, "that the crisis of my life has come!" Her aunt was not prepared for such a startling statement. However she managed to say quietly, "Something of importance must have happened, dear."

"Yes, Auntie, something very important to me." Cornelia then told at length of her lifelong friendship for Jimmie; how he had been almost a brother to her. She then related what he had said to her. There was something else to complicate matters. Isaac Amsden had shown such an interest in her lately; had singled her out for special attention everywhere they had met. She owned he was handsome, and she thought her heart beat faster when he was near her or even looked at her. She wasn't sure what was the correct thing to do in this situation.

"You see, Auntie, this is the critical time of my life."

Auntie saw that Cornelia was worked up over these momentous happenings, and needed to be quieted and soothed. So she began slowly: "Here are two young men, brilliant and handsome, both of excellent families. Each is well educated and has distinguished manners. Each is bound to be successful. Either would make a kind, loving husband that any woman could be proud of. So far, it would be hard to choose between them.

"But God has arranged these matters for us, for marriages are decided in heaven. He has put something into the hearts of young people that shows unmistakably the ones intended to be their mates. If they only will follow that signal and not decide too rashly; if they will not let their impetuosity destroy that signal. . . . I am able to talk to you on this subject because of a mistake I once made. I let my head and my will decide against my heart. I was as wilful and determined as my betrothed. We each should have given in a little. But, dear, do not try to decide now. You need a little time for these things to work out properly. Then my advice is, 'Follow your heart.' "

Cornelia listened closely to this sage advice, and a load seemed to lift from her spirits.

"Auntie, you have helped me more than I can tell you."[3]

CHAPTER X

Brevet Second Lieutenant James B. McPherson

In the years since James had first left for West Point, Russell had taken advantage of every spare moment to earn money. Such was his desire to assist James that, in spite of his aversion to physical exertion, he worked at any job he could find. Also, his determination to finish his own education was strong. He allowed nothing to interfere with these, his two great aims. During his vacation he worked in Ames's general store. He also helped Billy who, now seventeen years of age, had charge of their mother's farm. The boys raised extra stock; they planted every foot of ground in order to increase profits. Cynthia gladly helped them in the fields, knowing the ambitious program Russ had in mind.

Russell did his farm work mornings, often beginning at daybreak, for trade in the store was light then. He assisted Ames afternoons and evenings until dark, or by candlelight until ten o'clock, or until the last customer was served. He was always pleased when he could write to James saying: "Enclosed find $10. Whenever you want any money write me. I shall take pleasure in filling all orders from you as long as I have the money."

James wrote on September 18, 1852: "Much obliged for the

money you sent. I trust I can pay it back soon and with compound interest. The last two weeks of camp life were very pleasant and it was with feelings of regret that I assisted in 'striking the tents.' There was a satisfaction, however, in knowing that at the end of 10 months I could greet you all once more."

James, who had consistently led his class in his studies for two years, found the work of his last year more to his liking than that of any of his previous classes. He wrote to Russell, "I have commenced studying Engineering, Logic and Minerology. I think I shall like them all, particularly Engineering. It is the most practical and contains the most common sense of anything I have studied." Thus he was introduced to his chosen profession, the one that was to carry him to distinguished heights in the coming years.

Russell was James's chief confidant in his family and received frequent news of school and social life at West Point. He received the following letter dated October 1, 1852:

> I have the best office in the corps, that of Quartermaster, which excuses me from all Infantry drill, roll call, etc. If there were only a few ladies here I might have a glorious time walking with them after 4 o'clock while the other cadets are at drill. As it is, I spend that hour and a half in the Library.
>
> During Encampment I was Captain of the Corps, but the officers were made over and I was dropped a file or two on account of my being so un-military as to allow the first class to ride to Practical Engineering in an omnibus the last day but one we were in camp. I do not regret having done so although I got twelve demerits for it and was deprived of my appointment as Captain.
>
> The fact is, my class had a great deal more to do last Encampment than any other first class had to do before. We were kept busy from five in the morning till seven in the evening with very little intermission. We were obliged to walk two or three miles every day to Practical Engineering, starting at half-past ten and coming back

at one, when it was so hot as to singe the shirt on a fellow's back.

The last day we went, there was a large four-horse omnibus standing near the road that had just come up from Cozzen's Hotel and, as we past, the fellows decided they wanted a ride. They chartered the omnibus giving the driver $3.00 to take them out about two miles. Thirty-five Cadets got into it, and such another jolly noisy crowd I never expect to see. They seemed not only to fill the bus, but to cover it on top and hang from every available point.

I did not dare go into it myself as I was Squad Marcher of the class and I would have been put under arrest had I done so. And the only thing which prevented me from getting a more severe punishment for allowing it was my not being on the ground when the fellows got into the bus.

Friendly invitations from the boys for James to join them went unheeded, although he would like to have taken part in the unusual escapade. Nevertheless, he enjoyed seeing their antics almost as much as if he were indulging in them.

During this time, Isaac Amsden increased his attention to Cornelia, with the result that "the rapid beating of her heart in his presence," as she had confessed to her Aunt Abby, continued to increase until she was sure it was Isaac she loved. In the fall of 1852 they became engaged. She told all this to James in complete frankness and he, wishing only her happiness, asked that they always be friends as they had been. She wrote, "Yes, Jimmie, and Cousins too. I couldn't bear anything else." They were not blood relatives but, because of the close friendship existing between their families, Cornelia had delighted in the pleasant pretense. And so they continued.

Cornelia, of course, did not realize the restraint James would be under when with her, but his well-disciplined mind and will allowed him to play his part as he had in the past. Whatever his feelings in the matter, James gave no inkling. His love for learning and investigation was being satisfied by his studies in architecture, international law and jurisprudence, and especially by the practical side of engineering, which manifested itself in the construction of bridges, aqueducts and defenses.

His social life was not neglected. He wrote to Russ in November, 1852: "I had a serenading excursion the other night in company with 8 or 10 good fellows of my class. It was cold but our hearts were warmed with the sweet smiles and flashing eyes of the fair ladies of the Point. The collars of our heavy overcoats were turned up (not to exclude the music), and we went from place to place making the night merry with the sound of violin, flute, guitar and frosty voices."

In the same month, Emeline sent further home news: "Russell left for Miami University; the Methodists have sent for a bell; the cars on the new railroad are expected here Tuesday; the thrill they receive when they hear the shrill whistle of the locomotive each morning; she has 20 pupils in a log schoolhouse in Riley; Aunt Betsy died and Cousin Phoebe keeps house for Uncle William; Billy injured his ankle when his wagon, loaded with railroad ties, upset."

The long, cold winter was slowly retreating and the time for James's graduation from West Point was approaching. His family was resigned to the fact that none of them would be present for it. What money they could spare must be sent to James for the things he needed. He would come home on furlough shortly after that and they would have him to themselves for a time.

James began to sense the feeling he would have on leaving the school he loved so well. He wrote to Clemmy:[1]

"I have just returned from our last concert for this season and one piece in particular, 'Sounds From Home,' struck a sympathetic chord. The time is drawing near to bid adieu to my Alma Mater. . . . When I have fairly entered the Army there is no telling what duties I may be called upon to perform, or when I shall be able to obtain a furlough. And I may find, if I should happen to be stationed among the swamps of Florida, or be sent to fight the Comanches in Texas, that the honor for which I have been striving is an empty one after all."

In March, 1853, Emeline wrote to James:

> Ma wants you to write at once and let us know how much money you will need for graduation. She added some news items: The Universalist Church is nearly finished and they have their bell; it is delightful to hear the bells ringing every Sunday in Clyde. There have been some accidents on the railroads; one man was killed last week on the Tiffin and Sandusky R.R. by the giant cars running over him; several passengers were injured on the Norwalk and Toledo R.R. between here and Bellevue by a tree being felled as the cars were passing. Erastus Whicher left for parts unknown owing Ma $30. Sylvester Whicher has gone into the Tavern.

James wrote home on May 10, 1853:

> Three weeks till examination and at its close I will doff the Cadet and don the Brevet. It is not without some feelings of regret that I shall bid adieu to West Point. I have often thought there is not another place to be found equal to it in beauty; and there is not another place which possesses a greater degree of interest for Americans.
>
> Some British officers were here about three weeks ago examining into the discipline and other matters and I think they were deeply impressed.
>
> I can hardly determine when I shall be home. I may have to stay as assistant-instructor in Practical Engineering during Encampment and then take my furlough in the fall. I can spend a week or two at home between the 20th of June and the 6th of July.

In November, 1852, Cornelia Birdseye had gone to New York City to visit her Uncle Christie and family and stayed almost a year. It was Uncle Christie who had sent her the fairy tales and the music she loved. It was he who owned the large department store and who sent her beautiful materials for dresses and bonnets, and yards and yards of ribbons. Cornelia longed to browse through that great "Emporium," as it was called, and see for herself where all the lovely things came from. Her cousins, Mary and Sarah Christie, took her there and she toured and shopped to her heart's content. She had never before seen such a vast amount of beautiful silks, brocades, velvets and poplins. Shopping was one of the highlights of her visit.

James, who occasionally visited the Christies; liked to tease Cornelia about shopping in New York. "I thought Bosley's store in Clyde had about everything one could want," he said.

"Oh, Jimmie," she said, "I can't even find thread there the color I want. And as for dress material—"

"He carries good unbleached muslin," Jimmie broke in. "Yes, and some red flannel." The girls shrieked with laughter.

"Yes," replied Cornelia, "I could have a gown for the theater made of the muslin with a red-flannel fichu."

The Christies gave many parties for Cornelia. James was invited to them and he attended as many as he could. He also accompanied them to grand opera, where they heard Grisi and Mario and other great singers of that time. He concluded that he preferred opera to the theater, and from then on he heard it whenever he had an opportunity.

Cornelia and her cousins made plans for several social affairs in honor of James's approaching graduation from the Military Academy on July 1, 1853. While James regretted that no member of his family was able to be present, he was proud to have Cornelia and her cousins and Mrs. Robert Smith and Elizabeth Stem for his guests.

The ladies stayed at Cozzen's Hotel previous to and following the great day, and James had the happiness to escort them to many of the festive gatherings. They met his cadet friends and their relatives. There were many parties, balls and boatings.

On the great day a large crowd was present for the historic exercises. Seats had been placed on the green turf to accommodate as many as possible. The fifty-two graduates marched to their places to military music by the band and took seats near the speaker's stand. Secretary of War Jefferson Davis gave a spirited address, and Colonel Robert E. Lee, Superintendent and Commandant, presented each cadet with his commission as brevet second lieutenant. Each received his parchment in the order of his rank in class: James B. McPherson of Ohio was first; William P. Craighill of Virginia, second; Joshua B. Sill of Ohio, third; William P. Boggs of Georgia, fourth. Others in that class who became famous in the Civil War were John M. Schofield of Illinois, seventh; Philip H. Sheridan of Ohio, thirty-fourth; John B. Hood of Kentucky, forty-fourth.

"James returned to New York with his guests and visited a short time. While there he had two daguerreotypes made, one for Cornelia and the other he sent to his mother."[2]

CHAPTER XI

Advancement

Lieutenant McPherson was retained at the Military Academy in West Point for the year immediately following his graduation, as assistant instructor in practical engineering. This was the first time in the history of the academy that a graduate was at once given a teaching assignment there. James keenly felt the splendid compliment.

In the latter part of July, James was given a week's furlough, which he spent in Clyde. He regaled his family with stories of his graduation and other important happenings at the Point in which he was involved. As his time was short he did little visiting beyond a trip to Greensprings to the Robert Smith family. Although he enjoyed seeing his own people, he was a little impatient to return to West Point, where he was earning money. At last, his mind repeated, he could begin to repay his loved ones for the constant help they had given him.

Cornelia did not know the exact time of James's furlough. When she arrived home from New York in August and found him gone, she wrote to him:

"You do not know how disappointed I was when I got home and found you were gone. I had made so many plans for visiting and horse-back riding that it seemed no easy matter to forget them.

"After leaving New York City I was delayed 24 hours by the cars running off the track. . . . Henry Niles is bringing me a riding horse so I will have plenty of practice before you come."

After James got to West Point, during encampment and later in the year he was busy drilling the engineering class in war maneuvers in the morning; in the afternoon, instructing the first class cadets how to lay fortifications in the field and to build pontoon bridges.

He felt his responsibility to the cadets he was teaching and gave them his undivided attention. His skill and knowledge in the work brought him to the attention of older men who had worked on engineering projects in different parts of the country. Therefore he was chosen to be assistant to Major Delafield, who was assigned to the work of fortifying New York harbor and other strategic points along the Atlantic and up the Hudson River.

In November, 1853, he was given a leave of absence for seventy days by order of Colonel Robert E. Lee. He spent the first half of it at home in Clyde. He and Russell could now take train rides to see their friends in neighboring towns. They visited schoolmates in Norwalk whom they had not seen since their Norwalk Academy days. They attended parties in Bellevue and Greensprings. Parties in Clyde were infrequent. They were still considered too worldly and tainted with Satan.

Nevertheless, Cornelia decided to give a ball in her home for James on New Year's Eve. She did an unheard-of thing. She brought an orchestra from Sandusky to play for the dancing and singing. Guests came from Clyde and surrounding towns by train and were met by bobsleds. To the tune of dancing sleigh bells mingled with singing and laughter, the horses frisked along the mile and a half to the Birdseye home. Cornelia met the happy crowd and she was soon surrounded by billows of chatter and laughter. When she could be heard she said to them, "Aunt Abby told me she heard you coming fifteen minutes ago. What delayed you?" All looked surprised.

"That must have been when we left Clyde. It's taken us

about that much time to come. Is it possible she could have heard us then?" Darwin asked.

"It's possible, for the air is clear and still," replied James.

"I'll admit we were making a little sound," added Emma Smith.

"A little, did you say?" questioned Russell. The banter was kept up and soon all sat down to a bountiful supper. Dancing, interspersed with blindman's-buff, charades and other games, then followed in the large attractive rooms, which were gay with blazing fireplaces and dozens of lighted candles and oil lamps.

As the hour of midnight approached, the gayety became subdued. New Year's, in those days, following the puritanical custom transplanted to our shores, was observed somewhat like Christmas is now. Bacchanalian revels welcoming the New Year were as yet unknown. At midnight James, who was looking at his watch, observed, "We have entered a new year. May it bring us closer to God's designs for us." Everyone knew James's deep religious convictions.

Added Clemmy, "May it bring us our hearts' desires." Some of her friends, observing her soulful glance at James, thought they knew what *her* heart's desire was.

"May it fill us with love," said Emeline. Fred Vandercook gave her a look that meant, "My heart is full of love now."

Russell added in a grave manner, "May Dame Fortune be with us." The solemnity of midnight was vanishing and young hearts were resuming their normal gyrations. Best wishes for a happy year were exchanged all around, and sleigh bells were soon heard again returning home.

James finished his furlough in visiting his friends in New York State. Before leaving for the east, he discussed with his mother and sister the letters he had received; they persuaded him to save those of any importance. He had saved few of the letters he had received at West Point, and none from Russell, who had become a delightful letter writer. His mother kept all missives received from him, though after his death, she gave many of them to friends who wished some memento of him.

Lieutenant McPherson left for New York City to assume his new position in August, 1854. He wrote from the Engineer's Office there, October 21, 1854, to Mrs. Smith:[1]

> I can only leave you to imagine the pleasure I experienced in meeting Sam and Lucius and hearing from so many things about my friends at home whom I had not heard from in a long time. I have always been frank with you, Kate, and I must say that I not only felt disappointed but hurt because I had had but two or three letters from the Springs since I left last winter. Perhaps you have imagined that gay scenes and new faces have "turned my head" and caused me to lose all interest in those who are far away. Such is very far from being the truth. And it is not because I do not want to see you that I do not think of coming home this winter, but because my duties are such that it will be almost impossible for me to obtain a furlough.
>
> I am much pleased with my boarding house. It is located well up town in a delightful part of the city, and the boarders are persons of intelligence and refinement. Among them are William T. Sherman who is agent for a banker's firm in St. Louis, and Major John Bernard of U. S. Engineers. Sherman is a West Point graduate.
>
> I like the work here very much. Major Delafield is an excellent officer to serve under and is considered one of the most talented officers in the Corps, so that I shall have a fine opportunity to acquire sound practical knowledge.

In November, 1854, Lieutenant McPherson was absent two weeks from the city, having been sent to a Dutch settlement called "Schodac," thirteen miles from Albany, to make some surveys and to take some soundings in the Hudson River, together with various other duties connected with the improvement of the river navigation. On his return to New York he was given full charge of the work there, as Major Delafield had gone to Washington for four or five weeks.

McPherson's advancement was rapid. The ease with which he made friends and the pains he took to please his superiors marked him for a successful career.

In a letter to Robert Smith, December 13, 1854, he said:[2]

> I have found time to participate in some of the festivities and amusements of the City, and I will give you an account of one affair in which I was interested. A week ago tonight the St. Nicholas Society gave their anniversary dinner at the St. Nicholas Hotel to which I was invited. This society is composed of the descendants of the "Old Knickerbockers" and of those who were citizens of the State at the time of the Revolution, and number some of the best speakers and most talented men in the City among its members. The dinner was served in a style of magnificence I have never seen equaled and required a bill-of-fair half a yard long.
>
> After the cloth was removed and before the president donned his "three cornered hat," clay pipes with stems a yard long were brought in with plenty of Turkish tobacco, and soon many wreathes were circling around the heads of more than a hundred persons. At this stage of the proceedings the president arose, made a short speech and commenced reading the regular "toasts" of the evening which were received with cheers. The fourth toast was "The Army and the Navy of the United States," upon the announcement of which the cheering was most enthusiastic.
>
> In the midst of the excitement a salute was fired from a miniature "Dutch Fort." The band then struck up "Hail Columbia" and "Yankee Doodle," after which the president called upon your humble servant to respond.
>
> Here was a fix. However, I was not taken altogether unawares as I had a few minutes to think up something prompted by the spirit of the occasion. I gave it to them and was complimented very warmly. I did not dream before going there but what there would be some older officer present, but it so happened I was the only one.

Though taken somewhat unawares, James contrived to give a brief but interesting account of the part the Dutch settlers had played in the making of New York and in its defense. His intimate knowledge of those historical events surprised and delighted the crowd. James had a warm feeling of pleasure, not only because his talk was so well received, but because he had proved himself equal to the unexpected situation.

Shortly after this affair, James had received the news of the approaching marriage of Cornelia and Isaac Amsden. He had extended his heartfelt wishes to the couple for their happiness. She had sent a warm invitation to the wedding to James; he could not leave his work at that time but promised to visit them at their home in Bellevue when he had a furlough.

James, always disposed for friendly intercourse, did not permit Cornelia's marriage to make him downcast. He had many invitations to parties, and frequently allowed himself the pleasure of week-end visits to homes of people he had met.

Another marriage of great interest to him was that of his beautiful and only sister Emeline to Frederick Vandercook, who had kept the general store next to the McPherson home. The young couple went to housekeeping in Fremont and began what proved to be a successful hotel business.

Russell McPherson, who had obtained a position with the American Express Company in Cincinnati, still enjoyed writing to amuse James. On March 1, 1857, he wrote:

> MY DEAR BROTHER, Surprised to hear you had left New York. The place where you may be next located is, I opine, about as uncertain as all other future events. You must have had a touch of the "blues" now and then having been sent to such a little "Pea Patch" of an Island as you describe. Why, the very thought of such a thing would, I should think, fill the soul of a Metropolitan with the solitary horrors. I should think some morning you would find the little sand pile missing on your return from the Post Office, with the Delaware River flowing over it.
>
> By the way, Jim, how "Tempus does fugit." Here it

is two months since we parted in Cleveland. It seems like a day dream. That visit home was too pleasant. If I had not enjoyed it so well it would have lasted longer. When I remember all the good times we had I feel sad to know we cannot prolong them "ad infinitum and ad libitum." Ergo: I am human. Consider me a profound logician for I have proved myself to be what somebody never dreamed of.

My washing has been done at home since I left. I send up my valise with the dirty clothes and a dirty little letter once in two weeks, and in return receive clean clothes and a clean letter. I keep up quite a correspondence with that valise as a medium.

Ma has written three letters to me with her own hand and right good ones they were. Billy has sent me one. I told him I weigh 156 lbs. and that he would have to put into the pork and beans or I would soon be a larger man. He replied he weighed 165 lbs. Why, the boy will be a colossus if he keeps at that rate.

I have written no apology for not answering sooner but you would ask none if you could see me now standing up to the desk and twenty fellows behind me singing, "My Mary Ann," "Bolin' Around," and "Few Days," and raising the devil, generally. The fact is there is no place in the whole institution where a fellow can write on Sunday without interruption. I shall expect letter upon letter from you in rapid succession and I'll answer the best I can.

The monumental work of fortifying New York harbor and its approaches, and improving navigation in that area, occupied about three years. The New York papers of December 1, 1857, carried the story that a tour of inspection around the harbor was made by the Secretary of War, Major Delafield, Lieutenant McPherson and other officers.

CHAPTER XII

McPherson Goes to California

The end of the Mexican War saw the United States with a vast expanse of new territory which extended westward to the Pacific and south to the Rio Grande. This acquisition, the result of southern influence and bullying, caused varying degrees of concern or indignation in the North, and mild satisfaction or noisy jubilation throughout the South. "How many slave states can be carved from the new territory?" was the question that seemed to engross the attention of many southerners who were encouraged to settle in the new land, especially California, as some had settled in Texas.

But their plans to make a slave state out of California failed due to the discovery of gold there in January, 1848. News of the discovery spread rapidly and thousands of people made their way to San Francisco, which to them was California. Sailors left their ships to rot in the harbor, and men came from every state and from many countries, all seeking a share of the precious metal.

Not all of the Forty-Niners were miners, however. Many younger sons of prominent southern families flocked to San Francisco. They wished not only to make a fortune but also to use their influence in politics. They were, for the most part, well educated, some of them being lawyers who were well versed in practical politics relating to slavery. Then, too, there was a generous sprinkling of adventurers who knew many ways of fleecing a person who had money.

The number of fortune-seekers entering San Francisco steadily increased, and the air of restlessness that pervaded the town seemed to expand. People spent money freely, and many saloons and places of entertainment provided the shifting population with bawdy and noisy amusements. Crime became rampant and life grew cheap. At one time in the early 1850's there was at least one murder every day. Walking on the streets after dark became a dangerous venture. The better classes of people became alarmed at the rapid growth of lawlessness and decided that something must be done to make their city a place where people could live in safety.

Vigilance committees were formed to cope with the situation and after a period of several years managed to bring comparative peace and security to the city. The United States government had been studying the situation and saw that San Francisco was the outlet of a vast and rich country, and was fast becoming an important center of commerce, both national and international. It at length decided to fortify the harbors of San Francisco and Alcatraz Island.

In December, 1857, Lieutenant James B. McPherson was ordered to California to take charge of building fortifications in those harbors. He arrived there in January, 1858, having taken the long trip by way of the Isthmus of Panama. On January 10, 1858, he wrote to Mrs. Robert Smith: [1]

> Having become fairly established in what will probably be my home for some time to come, I hasten to inform you of my safe arrival here after a passage of twenty-six days. It being my first voyage at sea there were many things of interest connected with it.
>
> Arriving at Havana, the steamer stopped several hours and I took occasion to go ashore. Fortunately just as I landed, I met a friend who is a resident of the

place. This was a piece of rare good luck, as it obviated all necessity of my trying to speak Spanish. Under his pilotage I was enabled to see many of the celebrated places in a short time. The flowers, orange trees, cocoa and palm tree were to me objects of the greatest curiosity. Also the town with its imposing fortifications, its old and venerable buildings, narrow streets and swarthy inhabitants.

It was too early in the day for the dark senoritas to make their appearance. I visited the Captain General's palace, a magnificent looking building, having a little open square filled with the choicest flowers and fruits. Then I went to the Cathedral, a Mission structure hoary with age in which the remains of Columbus were deposited in 1797. The tomb is near the Altar and is monumental with his bust sculptured in marble.

Time flew rapidly and I was compelled to hasten on board the steamer and was soon on the way to Aspinwall. Here we took the cars for Panama occupying some four hours in crossing, a great improvement over what it was three or four years ago when it required as many days, half of which were consumed in poling up the Chagres River and the other half in alternately coaxing and beating a stubborn mule.

On this side I was fortunate enough to have one of the best steamers in the Pacific, viz. the "Golden Gate." The distance from Panama to San Francisco is almost 3600 miles so it is very important what kind of a steamer you have. I was twelve days in coming up.

Alcatraz Island looks very much as I had expected it did, being a small, rocky Island with bold precipitous shores, and distant about a mile and a half from the city. I have not had much time to travel about the country and see the sights though I expect in a few months to make one or two excursions, one back into the country to see the big trees and the gold diggings, and another to New Almaden to visit the quicksilver mines.

It can be seen that little escaped his observation and that every thing he saw was of interest to him.

When James arrived in San Francisco he was met by some of his officer friends who had been stationed there. Among them were Lieutenants George Elliott of Massachusetts, G. W. Custis Lee of Virginia, Steve Merchant of New York, J. G. Kellogg of Michigan, Major Hammond of California and others. All of these men had been appointed to assist him in his new work. They took him to his cottage in the Presidio, which was an army post on Fort Point overlooking the Golden Gate. There were other cottages there and a large officers' club.

Over a belated supper they spent time in bringing James up to date on news of their mutual acquaintances. Lieutenant John Hood was in Belknap, Texas. Lieutenant Prince had left for New York. Lieutenant Donelson was ordered to Utah to help quell the Mormons. John Schofield and Cyrus Comstock had teaching assignments in West Point. The talk turned to the vigilance committee.

"San Francisco has improved its manners somewhat since I came here four years ago," remarked Hammond. "I saw the viligantes string more than one culprit to a convenient tree."

Laughed Lee, "It's almost a Garden of Eden now."

"It still has a few serpents though," added Elliott.

"And a number of Eves to be tempted," put in Kellogg.

"Yes, they fall like the original Eve."

James queried, "Are all the ladies here as you have painted? I'll have to go back to New York if that's the case."

"No, indeed," said Lee. "I can introduce you to some beautiful ladies that you'll admire. I never saw one in New York to surpass them. You'd better stay." James agreed to do so.

They spent hours discussing the work that lay ahead of them and planned to look over the situation the next day. It was decided that the fortifications on Alcatraz would be made first. The government furnished them with a boat to be used on their trips to and from the island. Shanties were built there to house the men who did the manual labor, and an office for James and his assistants. The rocky place which presented so uninviting and dangerous an appearance was almost home to James and his men for more than a year. When they had finished, the place was practically impregnable, and the fortifications made there under McPherson's command are still intact.

Because of McPherson's position as chief of fortifications and because of his unusual bearing and friendly manner, he attracted much attention in the city. He was invited to assist in civic movements such as laying out new allotments and speaking at patriotic and other public affairs. He helped many an individual appeal. A number of the few letters that have been salvaged after the long years are notes of thanks from grateful people whom he assisted in some way.

Russell wrote from Cincinnati, February 2, 1858:

> MY DEAR BROTHER, I do not believe in ghosts or omens, nor can I read the future by the signs of the present times. But I confess I did feel considerable anxiety for your safety when the steamer arrived two weeks ago without bringing a letter from you. Happily the next steamer set everything right bringing glad tidings of great joy from the distant shores of the Pacific where the golden sun sheds its golden rays o'er the golden hills, plains, valleys and gorges of the golden land of promise. My "Pheelinx" which had been somewhat depressed became buoyant on the receipt of your letter.
>
> By the way, Jim, in your golden state everything must become by the action of sympathetic influences decidedly yellow. I should think that "Yeller Kivered Litterachure" would be immensely popular in such a country. I mean nothing of disparagement of your adopted State. On the contrary, I hold that yellow is incomparably better than blue, as the former always represents the sunny side. And with plenty of the yellow dust in your pockest you can always—most always—keep that side in view.
>
> I see by the paper that the Overland Surveying Party have made a favorable report respecting the new

> wagon road, having found no insurmountable difficulties on the route. You may look for me in San Francisco some time—I can't say when—approaching the Golden Gate over same wagon road, mounted on a camel, or donkey, or dromedary, for it don't make much difference which to either you or me, for it's Big Pig—root hog or die to a young man in search of adventures, who don't care a snap for Dame Fortune if she only sticks to him. Keep a good lookout just beyond the limits of the City if you want to see my advent. You will know me by the spectacles and by my industry in my search for a good looking man about your size.

McPherson received many letters and somehow contrived to answer them. The following give an insight into the friendly relationship he maintained with numerous people: E. M. Stotsenberg wrote from Wilmington, Delaware, "When I am smoking my cigar I often think I see you with the red ornamental cap, or perhaps the Delaware—christened old white hat covering your precious pate, marching over your rocky and sea-girt home, marking, describing, and directing, thinking of home and friends and glory."

John M. Schofield wrote from West Point: "I have got a big, big bouncing boy with a tremendous pair of lungs. His most remarkable feature is his nasal appendage. I have no doubt you find the climate of California very delightful. But fancy your little Island must be rather a dull place. Now if you only had a wife and BOY, wouldn't it change the color of things considerably?"

Russell wrote on March 1, 1858:

> I recently made the acquaintance of Lt. Thompson of Newport, Ky. On learning that I am your brother, he showed me marked attention, even went so far as to invite me to dine with him at his house. It is needless to say that the invitation was respectfully and firmly declined. Not because I was unwilling to gratify him but simply because I am averse to certain sequences always

inevitable when heterogeneous individualities meet. I avoid all social parties and decline all invitations to dine at private homes. Lieut. Thompson is well known here and honored as a true gentleman.

Last Friday night 350 U. S. soldiers passed through here enroute to Utah. If they can fight as well as they shouted then Brigham Young will catch h—— sure.

In the following letter James explains a matter that has caused him some worry:

My dear Russ,

Do you hear anything of Mr. Stem's people now-a-days? I have had only one letter from them since I left home in which they deemed to think I was losing some of my friendship for them. My last visit was unsatisfactory because of its shortness, and for some other causes which, I apprehend, exist more in the fancy than anywhere else. I am unconscious of any change of my feelings towards them and have ever entertained the warmest respect for the whole family.

But the truth is, some persons will persist in believing that I am engaged to one of the young ladies when the truth is, there is not and never was anything of the kind, and for five years I am trying to make them believe it. Knowing and hearing those reports, I may have been constrained and embarrassed at the Springs, and this is the ground on what they base their opinion that I am growing distant. Time, I trust, will make all things right.

Russell, who called his letters from James "dispatches from the War Department of Alcatraz Island," told him how highly they were valued and how they went the rounds. He added, "There was some talk of reducing salaries a month ago. I gave them to understand that my time was worth all they ever paid me and if they wanted me to quit it was the best thing they could do to cut me down about 20%. This they did not do and I don't know now as I ever shall quit this damned town unless it be to follow you."

James's grandmother, Lydia Slocum, wrote him the following letter on September 15, 17858: "In my loneliness I take my pen in hand to inform you of the death of your Grandpa Slocum. He departed this life Aug. 26 after a long and distressful illness which he bore with great resignation to the will of his Heavenly Father in that patience which I think is rarely met with. I am left a little longer to learn that this is not my home and to prepare to follow the loved ones."

McPherson's work on Alcatraz was steadily progressing. At first this required much planning, surveying, soundings and computing quantities of materials. He had been assigned four years for the project, which included, besides Alcatraz, Fort Point, Lime Point, Benicia, Lovell's Island and other places that required the protection that the exigencies of that time seemed to indicate. McPherson felt his responsibilities, and the trust that the government had placed in him was reflected in his utilization of every moment, day and night, in order that he might find the best method of working out his plans. His engineering skill was such that the day's work seemed like a pattern in which each of his men fitted each part, making the pattern complete. His kindly and helpful manner brought pleasure to the task at hand for all of his workers. The men were not underlings; they were friends with whom he freely discussed every phase of the work.

The United States surveying steamer *Active,* with Captain Alden, was at McPherson's service at all times while he was stationed in San Francisco. It took him and his officer workers to the island in the morning and returned them to the city late in the afternoon, sometimes at dusk. Their work was of absorbing interest to each man and was discussed whenever two or more of them were together, even at their social affairs, to the embarrassment of their ladies on more than one occasion.

McPherson's service and devotion to his country were the most important aspects of his life. Regardless of his interest in beautiful young ladies and his close association with society, duty came first with him at all times. He set aside the pleasures of life if they interfered in any way with what he considered his plain duty. At such times he seemed to treat himself with great austerity. On several occasions he refused a furlough which was due him in favor of some other officer who had a wife and family, or a business to look after. While he had great brilliance of mind, many of his successes came to him in large part through his application during the night hours to the problems confronting him. Indeed, some of his friends questioned the idea that he ever slept. Those closest to him knew that two or three hours of sleep were all he allowed himself when a matter of great importance lay before him.

A letter from Russell was a perfect "Balm of Gilead" to the spirits, as James had written. Russ tried to apply that balm by writing on October 1, 1858:

> Do you know that there are hosts of your friends in the Atlantic States who are dying to hear from you? Not a line has reached us via the Ocean Steamer, the Isthmus, or New York. Not a token or a word from the great Overland Mail Routes. I trust that all is well and by not writing yourself you seek to punish me for a like fault. . . .
>
> I went home Sept. 1st for two weeks. Visited your friends at the Springs who seem never to tire of asking questions about you. Robert Smith is living in his new house which is one of the best in the county. I was also at the celebration of Perry's victory at Put-in-Bay Sept. 10th. Steamer loaded to the guards with fair women and brave men (men are brave, you know, when drunk). The rolling drum, the roaring of the cannon, the strains of music from several brass bands and shouts of men astonished the Heavens. The wind blew, the petticoats flew, high as the knees and higher too.
>
> Since writing the foregoing I received your letter of the 20th and didn't know whether to destroy this and start over. But "as a bird in the hand corrupts good morals" and as "Evil communications are worth two in the bush," I have concluded to send it verbatim and lit-

> teratim. By these presents I command you to imagine that any sentence which censures you in the least for neglect is hereby made null and void.

The next important news that James received from his family concerned the wedding of his youngest brother. William (Billy) McPherson was married at Hartland, Niagara County, New York, December 2, 1858, to Miss Mattie Andrews of that town. They made their home with Cynthia for a time. Later Cynthia built the newer-style house on the pike facing East Street and went there to live. Billy and his bride remained in the homestead.

Russ wrote concerning the marriage: "Ere this reaches you our youngest brother will most likely be a steady, sober, industrious married man. Congratulate him. I shall. Marriage is the very thing for Bill, and for me, too, if I had a cool $100,000."

He adds: "If any man in San Francisco inquires after me give him a quarter. If any girl inquires after me don't have anything to do with her for I don't know any that are virtuous, and of such is the kingdom of Hades."

In the same month James B. McPherson received his first promotion in the army when he was given the rank of first lieutenant, proof that his work was satisfactory to the government.

The work that James and his men were engaged in was of deep interest not only to the citizens of San Francisco but to friends who visited them and wished to see the sights of the city, including its unusual fortification problems. These visitors were cordially received by James and his officer friends, who always extended them the hospitality of a host to his guests. Since no money had been advanced for such a purpose by the government, the officers were of necessity compelled to pay for the service. The following petition to Secretary of War Jno. B. Floyd by the officers explains their position:

> SIR,
>
> We, the undersigned, believing that a proper statement of the circumstances attending our official position as officers of the Engineer Corps stationed on the Pacific

Coast will induce you to consider formally our petition, do respectfully request that the permanent works on the Coast in charge of Engineer Officers may be designated as "double ration posts" for the following reasons:

First,—The cost of living and all other incidental expenses as compared with similar stations on the Atlantic Coast are at least 40% greater, making it necessary for us under ordinary circumstances to practice the most rigid economy in order to live upon our pay.

Second,—The fortifications for the defense of the Harbor are located in the vicinity of the City, the inhabitants of which very properly take a deep interest in their progress and not only visit them frequently but bring such of their friends, strangers in the City, who may be stopping for a short time and express a desire to see them. So that scarcely a week passes that we are not called upon to extend proper civilities to persons of standing and influence in the community in consequence of our official position.

Third,—Designating the permanent works as "double ration posts" will give us a small increase of pay which will to a certain extent compensate us for the extra expenses to which we are subjected while in charge of the construction of these works, and will simply be placing us on an equality with other officers in other arms of the service who are in command of important stations.

Russell writes to James on July 17, 1859:

I was home and found Billy in the calm delights and comforts of home with the wife of his bosom by his side. She is a good, healthy, sensible girl, possessed of a happy temper and very great affection for her husband.

Uncle Bill was married last fall, you know. You see, Jim, everybody marries except you and me. We don't because we have such queer notions about connubial felicity, and such extravagant ideas of what constitutes

> a respectable home establishment, and I have so little faith in some women's virtue and so little respect for any woman not above suspicion! And then everybody suspects everybody and nobody thinks anybody as good as somebody pretends herself to be,—so what the devil is a man going to do?
>
> Elizabeth and Lydia Stem spent the winter here with Mathias. I met them several times. Mrs. Robert Smith sent me a splendid bouquet about four weeks ago with a note saying she hoped the fragrance would remind me of home friends. I put the flowers in a glass and placed them on my desk where it remained until the flowers withered but I noticed the perfume still remained. It occurred to me that the perfume is to the rose what virtue is to a woman. Though she wither like the rose if virtue, that most heavenly of all perfumes, remains she possesses that beauty which fills the soul with gladness.

The two years since McPherson had begun his work on the fortification of San Francisco harbor were also marked with history-making events in the east. The agitation against slavery had grown as the Abolitionists increased their moral and political activity. A feeling of antagonism among different sections of the country seemed to be growing. In October, 1859, news had come that John Brown had seized the arsenal at Harper's Ferry and was going to arm the slaves. That act was denounced in every place where two or more southerners were collected.

When his execution was announced in December, 1859, their rejoicing knew no bounds. California wine flowed freely to enhance the hilarity, and even the ladies thought the occasion called for a stimulus for merrymaking.

Custis Lee, who had returned to the Engineer's office in Washington, wrote to James, January 4, 1860:

> I find that I look for California news with more interest than I do for that in this part of the world. Indeed, there is nothing in Washington of any interest except

> perhaps the proceedings of Congress, and they are frequently so disgusting a character that I never read them unless I hear that something special has been done. There is no speaker yet and but little chance of any being elected soon.
>
> - hope you had a refreshing New Years in San Francisco. I take it for granted you went to see all your acquaintances, viz: every man, woman and child in San Francisco.

Every letter that James received in 1860, preceding the election, mentioned the coming political campaign and the turmoil that was expected over the question of slavery. Dissatisfaction with Buchanan's action or lack of action on the subject was the prevailing attitude, particularly in the North. "James Facing-Both-Ways," as the President was dubbed, could do little to solve the difficulties that arose in Congress.

Russell wrote to James on the subject on January 7, 1860:

> We are now about to begin the Presidential campaign which is bound to be the most exciting one ever witnessed. Lincoln's prospects are good for carrying every free state. The John Bell party is very small but it is expected to make up in noise what it lacks in numbers. It may make a good showing if the "Charleston Split" in the Democratic party is not healed up at Baltimore. Upon the healing of this split depends the very existence of the Democratic party.
>
> Douglas is bound to be a candidate but he can't be elected. The South will not trust him and he has lost favor in the North by being too obsequious toward the South. You know Benton is reported to have said that Douglas never could be President because his coat tails hung too near the ground.

Lieutenant Steve Merchant wrote from Astoria on January 8, 1860:

"My dear Mac, The Union is gone. The North and South are

both perfectly rabid and Christian forbearance is nowhere to be found."

Cyrus Comstock wrote to James from West Point on February 11, 1860:

My dear Mac,

With the snow a foot deep and rapidly falling, the thermometer about 20 degrees, time Sat. 3 P.M., class reports in and the toils of the week ended, with my face to you and my back to the fire; if under such a conjunction of favorable planets I cannot write, my birth must have been under an ill-omened star.

You may know I am here in Philosophy, a post which I believe you once had the honor of philling. Your class is well represented here—Graighill, Schofield, Symonds; Symonds is a fiery Republican. Fortunately everyone at the mess is a Northerner but DuBarry or we would have some hot times. All in all, the atmosphere at the Point is calm and salubrious. Who knows when we shall have a storm?

CHAPTER XIII

James Meets Emily

James B. McPherson was now in his thirty-second year. As yet no young lady had succeeded in effacing the image in his mind of his youthful neighbor and "cousin." He had met many a lovely girl to whom he was attentive and courtly. They were all "young ladies" whom he considered to be on a higher plane than members of his own sex. On the other hand he was responsible for many feminine sighs and heart flutterings, as he was considered one of the most eligible young men in San Francisco.

He met a young woman in the spring of 1859 at a party given by Senator and Mrs. William Gwin. She was Emily Hoffman, a Baltimore belle, who had come from that city to be with her sister Sophie. Sophie Hoffman had married Louis McLane, whose father had been ambassador to England and later a member of President Andrew Jackson's cabinet. They were married about the time gold was discovered in California and were among the southerners who went to that country to make their home. They arrived in San Francisco in the early 1850's and helped to establish the upper stratum of society that remained prominent many years.

"Mrs. McLane became the mother of eight children and she asked her sister to come to her assistance in guiding her brood and also in her social duties. So Emily took the long trip to California, by way of the Isthmus, and remained there a few years."

When James was introduced to Emily by her sister, he little thought that the small, straight, attractive young woman would dominate his world for the rest of his life. Her deep-blue eyes gazed into his somewhat puzzled face.

"Do I look like someone you have known?" she inquired.

"You must pardon my evident puzzlement, but why have I not met you before? But," he added slowly, "of course you must be newly arrived."

"Not so recently."

"We keep track of the new arrivals, but you have escaped detection, it seems."

"Yes," she said smiling, "I've managed to conduct myself fairly well so far, so I haven't been caught. But seriously, I asked Sophie to let me have some rest. When my friends in Baltimore knew I was planning to go west, they feted me to such an extent that I was almost a physical wreck; but I thought the four weeks on the steamers would rest me completely. To my great disappointment, instead of getting rested I got *mal der mer,* as I am not a very good sailor."

"You, too," he replied. "I can sympathize with you, for I know all about it. I found it anything but restful. You are feeling well now, I hope?" he asked.

"Yes, indeed, and ready for action. As a landlubber I can dance and ride and do other pleasant tasks."

Her vivacious spirit and ready repartee caught his admiration. "May I have the pleasure of the next dance?"

She nodded. He took her hand and gently drew it through his arm as they walked to the ballroom. James continued, "Sophie didn't tell me her sister was here. I'll have to have an understanding with her."

"But she told me about you, so I was looking for you."

"Were you prepared for the worst?" asked James.

"Her descriptive powers are excellent and—"

"Yes?"

"I'm not disappointed."

"That's all I can ask—now."

With that they entered the courtly measures of the Virginia reel, through which they moved with grace and evident pleasure.

They were partners in other dances that night, during which they found they had many interests in common. They read French authors; they could converse in the language without too much difficulty. They enjoyed singing and were devotees of grand opera. When the McLanes were leaving, James accompanied Emily to the carriage. He asked permission to call upon her, to which she readily assented. As he gazed after the receding carriage he wondered if Fate had visited him that evening in the person of Emily Hoffman. He tried to recall her face but could only remember that her eyes were very blue.

Thus began a companionship that grew in fervor during the rapidly passing months, when they were seen together frequently. He visited her regularly at the McLane home on fashionable Bryant Street and escorted her to social affairs, lectures, concerts. He walked with her to church—the Protestant Episcopal—and carried her Book of Common Prayer. His own Book, which bears evidence of usage, he purchased in New York before sailing for San Francisco.

James wrote to his mother about Emily: "You will love her as I do when you know her. She is intelligent, refined, generous hearted and a Christian. This will suit you as it does me, for those qualities lie at the foundation of every pure and elevated character."[1]

James had finished fortifying Benicia and Lime Point and, in May 1859, had returned to San Francisco. Funds for further work were depleted. In June Congress appropriated $50,000 for Fort Point and $25,000 to finish the work on Alcatraz. It was estimated that another year would be required to make the harbor safe from attack. James was happy to remain in San Francisco, although every letter he received from the East had some disquieting news.

James and his officer friends took advantage of the time before Congress voted money for further work on the harbor. They issued an invitation to a ball to be held at the Presidio on May 2, which was the tenth anniversary of the establishment of the United States Army Post on the old Spanish reservation. They invited all of their friends in San Francisco.

"Society in all its finery gathered at the Plaza that night on foot or in hacks to enter the waiting omnibuses for the long ride to the Post. The ball was a brilliant affair. The grand march was led by Surgeon Keeny and his wife, and the rich gowns of the ladies and the military uniforms made a gorgeous scene."[2]

Emily Hoffman with the McLanes and their friends were among the gay crowd that danced and played games that night at the Presidio. James contrived to have several dances with Emily as well as a stroll through the garden, although his duties as host did not appear to be neglected.

Russell wrote to James from Clyde, July 8, 1860:

> Here I am at home on a two weeks furlough striving very hard to amuse myself but with indifferent success. I had arrangements made for a fishing excursion to the Bay today. Billy, Joe Stevenson, Doc Eaton and myself were to form the party. Each one was to provide himself with fishing tackle, a basket of provisions, live frogs for bait, and a baggage wagon to bring home the fish. . . . But this morning at an early hour a dismal, damp rain set in wetting our out-door prospects. Of course it is to be regretted that the morning was wet. In fact, damn aggravating.
>
> I have some thought of preparing a Lincoln speech for the opening of the Republican wigwam, but am deterred from so doing by my inability to solve this question: Will not my speech damage my reputation more than it will benefit the party? Certanly, the party would derive very little benefit from any speech that I can make. But then, my reputation is at so low an ebb that there is nothing I can do to lower it in the estimation of the public. Hence, I do not think a speech by me would produce any effect on either side. I will not make the attempt.

CHAPTER XIV

The Threat of War

By this time the East and the West had been drawn closer together by the establishment of the Pony Express and the Overland Mail Route. Mail steamers to New York were now sailing twice a month. San Francisco was spreading out to the east and south, and many great mansions were built on the new streets. Larger and more ornate theatres and dance halls and music auditoriums appeared in order to satisfy the demands of the pleasure-loving people. Music and dancing and lively games were necessary to match the exuberant spirits of the time. The air was charged with the zest of youth; the town was young and the greater number of people were youthful. Everyone sought diversions, and gayety prevailed.

Added to that, the restive question of slavery was of paramount interest and importance, and it kept the southerners in California in a ferment of excitement. The compromises between the North and the South appeared to settle nothing; indeed, the Dred Scott Decision of 1857 had opened the question wider than ever. Threats of secession had already been heard, but most people thought them mere talk. However, it provided a topic of conversation among all classes of people and, though society appeared to be as gay as ever, there was an undertone of disquietude. The southern leaders kept in close touch with the political situation in the East, and tried to appear not too concerned over trends of events.

When McPherson and his workers had an hour of leisure they discussed the political news that came regularly from the East. In 1860 the news became more and more ominous until threats of war hinted. McPherson wrote to an eastern friend:

> I have felt a good deal of interest in politics since I have seen the efforts which have been made to form a sectional party—a party with but one idea—and that one calculated to awaken a feeling of animosity from one extreme of the Union to the other, the fatal effects of which neither you nor I can predict. When I see men who are endowed with superior powers of mind, and occupying high stations, putting forward their utmost energies to excite dissension, and not only dissension but absolute hatred between the different sections of our country, I feel it is time they were shorn of their strength and rendered powerless to commit evil.
>
> When men like Salmon P. Chase, whose position gives him influence, gets up before a public assembly and declares that there is a deep feeling of hatred between the North and the South, it is time that all truthful men should act to defeat the schemes and machinations of such demagogues. The time has come when good and true men must rally around the Constitution and the Union, and stay the tide of sectionalism and fanaticism which is spreading throughout certain parts of the country.

While war seemed remote, the increasing tension foreboded the coming of a crisis. Said James, "If it comes I shall take part in it." There was but one idea in his mind regarding the situation: "The Union must be preserved at all costs." He believed the furore was caused deliberately by a few selfish leaders who refused an honest compromise. His southern friends in San Francisco could discuss the subject with him because he talked in a reasonable manner on it.

They knew his stand and that was: *"The Union comes first. It must be preserved."* Other matters must be adjusted to human rights. The point is that everyone must give up something in order to preserve the Union and peace. His plan for a peaceful solution to the question was for the government to buy the slaves and set them free. Their former owners could hire them, if they wished, at a cost not much greater than the expense of their support had been.

Seriously James and his friends discussed the plan and every phase of it. The estimated cost of such a procedure would be trifling, they thought, compared to the expenditure of men, money and the inevitable ill will in the event of a war. McPherson was confident that if those ingredients of a plan could be discussed without the heat of passion and with an honest desire to find a solution, a peaceful settlement could be made.

It would, of course, take time and infinite patience to adjust the varying ideas of the few for the good of the many. Problems just as difficult had been solved in our Constitutional Convention in 1787, problems that seemed about to wreck the Assembly. But wise, cool heads were always there to propose some solution to the immedite difficulty.

Where were the wise, cool heads in the years preceding the Civil War? It appears that pride and greed had eradicated the natural American tendency to fair play.

In the meantime the presidential campaign was becoming more exciting and acrimonious. The action of the South if Lincoln should be elected was the uncertain factor that almost paralyzed the nation. President Buchanan wavered between the demands of the North and those of the South until the country scarcely had a President.

Billy McPherson wrote to James, October 1, 1860: "I sent you one of our County papers, Jimmie. These are exciting times in the way of politics. We have been favored with some of the best speakers in our wigwam. Governor Denison spoke one day last week. We all think Honest Abe will win. Saw and heard Stephen A. Douglas the other day."

James had a letter from Cyrus Comstock, who continued the political discussion:

> For fear that in the coming political excitement there may be non-intercourse established between East and West as well as North and South, I avail myself of the present opportunity to assure you of my most distinguished consideration, etc.
>
> I wish this coming election were over. The talk of secession may be all wind but it has a dreary sound. The Adjutant General of Virginia, it is said, is in New York with $500,000 for the purchase of arms. South Carolina has or is about to call a convention to consider Heaven knows what, and all this looks bad. I suppose there is little doubt of Lincoln's election and, in that case, the South will either collapse like a bag of wind or act.

Abraham Lincoln was elected President of the United States on November 6, 1860. Many citizens were filled with apprehension as to the outcome. "What will come of it?" wrote Comstock at West Point. "That is the question that we all ask and no one answers. All Southerners here are conservative and say the South is insane. But they also say if their own state secedes they will join her. I hope the Southern states will expend their wrath in conventions, and conclude to ride even if they do not hold the reins."

Custis Lee gives his views to James in a letter from Washington, November 17, 1860: "I have personally no apprehension in regard to the administration of the Republican party; but I think the signs of the times are strongly in favor of dissolution of the Union. I am in hopes that the everlasting Negro question may be settled on some fair basis and that matters will all turn out well yet; but the chances are against it."

In the month following the election of Lincoln the secession convention, which met at Charleston, South Carolina, voted unanimously that she was no longer a member of the Union. Because of this act, Major Anderson, who was in command of troops in Charleston Harbor, secretly moved them from Fort Moultrie to the stronger Fort Sumter. Such a course had not been anticipated by the Secessionists, who were enraged by the clever move. The merchant ship *Star of the West,* in trying to send provisions to the garrison on Fort Sumter, January 9, 1861, was fired upon and forced to put back. The dreadful suspense almost paralyzed the North, where the President seemed unable to make decisions of any kind. The only activity shown was in the South, where, before February 1, six other states had seceded. They were Mississippi, Florida, Alabama, Georgia, Louisiana and Texas.

CHAPTER XV

James Is Sent to Boston

In the early morning of April 12, 1861, Fort Sumter was fired upon by the Confederates under General Beauregard, the garrison returning the fire. The duel continued during the twelfth and part of the thirteenth, when terms of evacuation were agreed upon. That contest marked the beginning of the Civil War and put an end to all peace plans and negotiations.

Russell wrote to James:

> Since I last wrote to you everything that concerns me as an individual goes on much the same; but as an American citizen everything has gone or seems going to the devil. In this damnable business of secession the wretched state of South Carolina took the lead with the sympathy and encouragement of your old friend Jim Buchanan. His complicity in the matter raised such a storm of indignation in the North that he at once changed his tactics, and instead of letting the disaffected states withdraw without opposition, determined to protect the government property at all hazards.
>
> If those states want to go, then LET THEM GO! There are already six states out of the Union, or claim to be

> out. They do not disdain to avail themselves of the United States mail facilities nor neglect to hold on to all government money nor to get all they can.

After the fall of Fort Sumter had shocked the North into a realization of what the South meant to do, McPherson wrote to his mother:

> My mind is made up and I see that I have but one duty to perform, and that is to stand by the Union and the support of the general government. I was educated at the expense of the government, received my commission and have drawn my pay from the same source to the present time. I think it would be traitorous for me, now that the government is really in danger, to decline to serve, and resign my commission.
>
> Not that I can expect any service of mine can avail much; but such as it is, it shall be wielded on behalf of the Union.

The fall of Fort Sumter caused great uncertainty in San Francisco. How would California go? Groups of solemn-faced men stood in front of the newspaper office, where news bulletins were written on blackboards. James and Senator Gwin stood there discussing the affair and each one put the blame upon the hot-headed politicians in the seceding states, saying, "They acted too hastily." Some of the southerners had been hinting at the possibility of California's seceding, but their main object was to fathom the sentiments of the people.

A mass meeting was called to decide, if possible, the prevailing attitude of the city. Several thousand citizens assembled near Market Street and listened to speakers, most of whom urged loyalty to the Union.

Finally a young man named Thomas Payne gave a stirring and impassioned talk against secession. Among other things he said: "Some of you here are kin to the men who suffered at Valley Forge, or at Saratoga, or at Yorktown in order to give us a nation. Would George Washington consent to see it divided?

Or Paul Revere? Or any minute man who spilt his blood at Lexington or Concord?" The great wave of applause that followed his speech showed plainly that Union sentiment prevailed in San Francisco, and that meant California.

McPherson was deeply touched by the patriotic fervor evinced by Payne. His whole being responded to the speech with a greater desire than he had ever felt to devote himself to his country's cause. He wrote to the Department of Engineers in Washington offering his services to the government.

This was something he had been considering doing for some time, thinking he might better his chances for promotion in the army. This speech, together with the unexpected and almost incredible act of war which occasioned it, made it his imperative duty to write at once. He received an answer saying that he had been made captain of the infantry. While that was not the position he desired, he decided to accept it, thinking that it would lead to the work for which he had been trained.

These political happenings had a direct effect upon the romance of James and Emily, who were planning to be married soon. If war should come, James would in all probability be called into service in the East. All angles of the case were discussed, and the McLanes urged them to marry at once.

"In the meantime, Emily received a letter from her mother forbidding her to marry a Northerner. All her family in Baltimore were opposed to it. With the exception of the McLanes, they were rabid Southerners."[1]

Another letter from her mother told her to come home at once. This was a source of grief to Emily, who, though very much in love with James, did not wish to displease her people. Sophie McLane wrote her mother that she still *needed* Emily's help, so she was allowed to stay.

This romance and its attending difficulties were known to the friends of the young couple, most of whom thought, like the McLanes, that they should be married. It received almost as much attention from them as did political affairs in the East. In fact, it appeared that those affairs were the main cause of this trouble in faraway California.

James thought Emily should decide what to do. He would not urge her to go against her people. So it was decided to let things go on as they were for a while. Perhaps there would be some peaceful solution of the political turmoil, which, in turn, would help to smooth out their difficulties.

In July McPherson was notified that he had been made captain in the Corps of Engineers, and was ordered to report to Washington at once.

He and Emily and their friends were pleased with this promotion, and yet—the love situation seemed as far from being solved as ever, and the lovers as undecided on what to do. While James and Emily sat together in the McLane parlor the night before he left San Francisco, they tried to console themselves with the thought that the war would be of short duration; he would soon return to her.

James thought that his position in life would be much better in the East than in California, as he felt that he had a fine chance to rise in his profession; there would be need of many military engineers. He then could give his bride more of the comforts and luxuries he wished her to have. Emily, knowing his ambition for her as well as for himself, encouraged him in his new work although her heart was filled with forebodings. They tried to be cheerful but their hearts were aching.

James left San Francisco on August 1, 1861. He wrote while on the steamer that took him away from San Francisco and his sweetheart:

Sunday, Aug. 4, 1861.

MY DEAREST EMILY

You cannot imagine how much I miss you, though each hour is but adding to the distance which separates us. As I take up your picture and look upon it I feel that you are with me and that a kind Providence will watch over us both and enable me, ere many months, to retrace my steps towards you, when we shall meet never more to be separated.

As I stood on the deck of the steamer last Thursday

morning looking toward the house that contained the dearest treasure on earth for me, I felt that I would give all that I possessed or ever hope to possess if I could but fly to you and say, "The task is done, dearest, and henceforth we will travel life's journey hand in hand." But it was impossible. The steamer was under way and the last visible cord which bound us to the shore was cut off.

But I thank Heaven every day and hour of my life, dearest Emily, that there are invisible cords stronger and more enduring than any ever made by hands which bind me to you; cords which will withstand the fury of the tempest, the rude shock of battle, and the allurements of an active, exciting life, and cause me to return to you with a heart overflowing with love and devotion. God knows, my dearest Emily, if it will be in my power to do so. This is what sustains me while I am writing and enables me to picture a future with you radiant with happiness.

As you are aware, the steamer after leaving the wharf was delayed a couple of hours waiting for some firemen, so it was half-past twelve before we rounded North Point. As we passed Sucigys Wharf, some persons were standing there waving their handkerchiefs and, although the distance was so great we could not recognize them, Captain, Dr. Hart and myself waved ours in return. I hope they were friends and perhaps not, but at all events I felt so kindly towards everyone in San Francisco that it did not make any material difference who they were. . . .

When James arrived in New York on August 30, he received his commission as captain in the Corps of Engineers. He notified the Department in Washington of his arrival and received orders to report there at once. At the War Department he was ordered to go to Boston. He was to have charge of the forts in Boston harbor; he also had to recruit a regiment of miners, sappers, and engineers for the Engineering Department. An officer of his training and ability was not needed for such work. In fact, a non-commissioned officer could have done it. James, however, thought it would not take long to get the required number of men. He left at once for Boston.

James's work of recruiting in Boston and vicinity progressed very slowly, and as he was anxious to get into active service, he became impatient and disgusted. His separation from Emily added to his discontent, and his letters to her and to others show his feelings. He received a letter from Russell, who, knowing the difficulties he was having with enlistments, said:

> I would enlist to-morrow and do some tall fighting for my country but I am told that these kid-gloved, be-spectacled young men won't do for privates, and don't know enough to discharge the duties of a Captain with credit to myself and honor to the service, and I have not enough influence with the War Department to get the appointment of Major General.
>
> Now you smile because this talk reminds you of what a large majority of the men say whom you ask to enlist in your company of sappers and miners. How the in-firmities do multiply! I mean that particular kind that renders a man unfit for military duty.
>
> I learned through the pony express that you sailed from San Francisco about the first of August, and I went home on the 30th of August hoping to meet you there but did not hear a word from you until September 12. My furlough had then so nearly expired that I had not time to make the trip or I certainly would have made it for the express purpose of seeing you. I may be able to get away for a few days next month.

James and Emily sent their letters to each other through the Pacific Mail Steamship Company, which Louis McLane had helped to establish. Steve Merchant, who handled them in the New York office, delighted in forwarding them. Steve, who had been assistant to James at Alcatraz, wrote: "I am rejoiced! You know my rejoicings are silent ones. There's where I differ from you in display of passion. I hope you will be fully repaid for your loving glances at your pale-featured friend. Tremulous too in the repeating of the better or worser, and richer or poorer! I enclose two letters received from her. You can have a quiet, loving time tomorrow and, a-la-Thackery, smoke over it, too, to your heart's content."

Lieutenant George Elliott, who took McPherson's place in San Francisco, wrote, on October 29, 1851:

> Dear Mac,
>
> I went last night to see Miss Emily. She was quite well and in pretty good spirits considering (as I inferred from what she told me) that you had written such low spirited letters from Boston. Of course they have a depressing effect on her, and I would hint that no matter what you feel (and I know you must be blue enough) you ought to write the liveliest sort of letters to her.
>
> Keep a stiff upper lip, Mac, and all will yet come right. I don't blame you though, for I know that I would under your circumstances, feel badly enough. Don't say anything of this to Miss Emily for I told her I would tell you she is as lively as a cricket.

James continued in the business of recruiting around Boston and his dissatisfaction with results increased. In November he wrote to General Halleck in St. Louis explaining his situation. The two had been intimate friends in San Francisco, and Halleck had recently been made a major general in the Department of Missouri, succeeding General Fremont as military commander of that area.

McPherson had talked to Captain Blunt, one of Halleck's staff members, who was in Boston recovering from the effects of having been thrown from his horse.

He told Halleck:

> I have just seen Captain Blunt and in conversing with him, find he is perfectly willing to exchange stations with me if it can be effected. He thinks it will be weeks

before he will be well enough to ride horseback and perform duties in the field, although he could look after the forts in this harbor and attend to the recruiting of one of the Engineer companies. I told him I would write you on the subject and see if the exchange could be made.

When I came from California I was anxious to get into active service. I felt somewhat disappointed on being ordered up here, though I consoled myself with the thought that I could raise a company in a month and be back in two months at the outside. But recruiting of the regular service is terribly slow owing to the strong inducements held out to Volunteers by the State. At the rate I am going, it will take at least four months to enlist the full complement of men.

Can you not, General, arrange so that I can get into active service somewhere? By so doing you will confer a great favor on

Yours truly,
JAMES B. MCPHERSON

Since James wished to enter active service when he applied for a position in the East, it is easy to understand his great disappointment in the work assigned him. General Halleck, who had been having difficulty in selecting efficient officers for his department from the hundreds who were pressing him for a position, was pleased with McPherson's appeal for "active service somewhere." As commander of the Department of Missouri, he now asked McPherson to join his staff as aide-de-camp, also as assistant chief engineer, and ordered him to report to him at once.

McPherson, overjoyed at this sudden elevation, hurriedly made his preparations to leave Boston. He checked out of his hotel on November 22, 1861. En route to St. Louis he made two stops: one in New York to purchase necessary military accouterments for his new position; the other in Clyde to visit his mother, grandmother and other relatives.

News of his coming home had preceded him, and all the

family had gathered to greet him. This was his first visit to them since he had left for California in December, 1857. Four long years it was to them at home—to those whose thoughts and actions were motivated by the news they received of what James was doing. Emeline and Fred, with their little Emma, whom Jimmie had named, and their baby boy were there. Russell had made a flying trip from Cincinnati to see his idolized brother.

"I dropped everything and left when I learned you were to be here," said Russ, "and I don't care a damn if they give my job to someone else."

"They probably won't," replied James. "The war is making men scarce in business and in all lines of work as the government calls for more."

Russell, wishing to keep the conversation in a light tone and away from the topic that was uppermost in the minds of everyone, said, "Do you mind if I try on your hat and gauntlets? If they look well on me, I may apply for a position as lieutenant colonel in the army."

James obligingly handed them to Russ, who donned them and tried to assume a military air.

"Not bad, brother," said Jimmie. "You might make it if you get a horse that will match up."

"Horse!" exclaimed Russ. "Now, Jim, you know damn well I never could stay on a horse. We are incompatible. They don't understand my unusual characteristics."

Billy broke in, "He means a horse doesn't care for his unusual weight."

Russ looked at Billy appraisingly and questioned, "Would you by any chance be speaking from experience?"

Billy, who was much heavier than Russ, answered, "It could be possible if I ever had the nerve to try to get on a horse."

Everyone enjoyed the bantering the brothers indulged in when together. It seemed like the old days.

But all were anxious to hear James tell of his experiences. He told them more about his sweetheart, whom he had described as his perfect ideal in letters home, and of the difficulties they had met when they planned to marry. His new position had worked almost a miracle on his attitude toward life. He was no longer blue; he was almost gay as he related some of his happenings in "wicked San Francisco" as well as in "self-righteous Boston."

He tried to quiet his mother's fears in regard to the war by saying it shouldn't last more than a year; that the South, by quick action, had almost stupefied the North in its initial advantages; the North was now aware of the kind of fighting it must do and was preparing for it; it had greater resources than the South and could fight years if necessary; the next few months would see a great change.

McPherson reported to General Halleck on December 1 and immediately received his appointments as aide-de-camp with the rank of lieutenant colonel, and as assistant chief engineer. He was ordered to make tours of inspection in Missouri, to establish recruiting stations, and to try to find the strength of the rebel General Sterling Price. He also was to indicate the best places to post troops to defend the state. His tours kept him away for days at a time and he always brought back valuable information.

In the meantime, General Halleck was organizing his forces as fast as the volunteers were enlisted, and pushing his preparations so as to be ready for the movement south. General Ulysses S. Grant commanded the district around Cairo and Commodore Foote had his gunboats there. The rebels had a strong force below Cairo and they also held Forts Henry and Donelson. In those places, without doubt, would be heavy fighting.

CHAPTER XVI

Combat Duty

1. Opening the Mississippi Campaign

By January, 1862, General Grant had gained the attention of the public by successfully maneuvering a small expedition to capture Belmont on the Mississippi. It was the only important gain made by the North since the opening of the war, and it won for Grant the reputation that caused Halleck to place him in charge of the movement south to open the Mississippi, as well as the Tennessee and Cumberland rivers. The immediate objectives were Forts Henry and Donelson.

General Halleck, who retained his headquarters in St. Louis, transferred Colonel McPherson to General Grant's staff as chief engineer of the army.

Throughout January, General Halleck had been getting his forces in readiness, and by February 2, transports and gunboats under Flag Officer Foote were transferring Grant's troops to points near Fort Henry on the Tennessee River. On the sixth the troops moved toward the fort in a heavy rainstorm which made the roads almost impassable. But the guns from the fort and those on Foote's gunboats carried on a bombardment while Grant's army was slowly advancing on muddy wood roads. The rebel General Tilgman saw he could not hold out and ordered his men to retreat to Fort Donelson. He then surrendered to Commodore Foote, and the Union flag was hoisted over Fort Henry.

The next day, Colonels McPherson, Webster and Rawlins went on board the *Carondolet,* one of the gunboats, with a company of troops and, under instructions from General Grant, proceeded up the Tennessee River and destroyed the bridge of the Memphis and the Bowling Green Railroad.

On returning they hastened to Fort Donelson, which was situated on the Cumberland River twelve miles east of Fort Henry. Before Grant sent his troops there, McPherson and his engineers reconnoitered the country between the two forts in order to find the best places to deploy them. When Grant's men arrived from Fort Henry, they at once took up positions already assigned them. It was a masterpiece of engineering and showed McPherson's natural ability to place men in battle. He also made a detailed map of the fort and its approaches that proved invaluable in the investment.[1]

On February 8, the First Division, General J. A. McClernand commanding, moved under the guidance of Colonel McPherson and took positions on the road and near Fort Donelson. Gunboats approached the fort and engaged the water batteries. In terrible weather, with snow and sleet falling, and with insufficient supplies, the troops kept up fighting until General Buckner capitulated on February 16.

Because of exposure and overexertion, McPherson became ill with a throat ailment and was forced to spend three weeks in St. Louis for treatment.

General Grant made special mention of McPherson in his report to General Halleck. His services in both engagements were recognized by a nomination for brevet major of engineers to date from February 16, 1862.

The people in the North were wildly enthusiastic over the surrender of Fort Donelson. It was the first major victory gained by the North, and many people thought the war was ended. A few sources, in their wild enthusiasm, mistakenly called it the most important battle in American history. Russell wrote to James:

> I received your letter dated St. Louis last Sunday, and it was the first positive proof I had of your safety. There never has been during my recollection such great rejoicing as on the reception of the news of the surrender of Fort Donelson. As a good Union man, I was bound to go in with everybody else and help to celebrate the victory, but I could not give full vent to my enthusiasm until assured of your safety. The letter gave me that assurance and I was then perfectly happy.
>
> Jim, I can find no words to express exactly what I feel when I bring to mind the glorious victories achieved by our gallant troops at Henry and Donelson, the last the greatest and most important military triumph that ever took place on this continent.

Mrs. Catherine Smith wrote: "I cannot withhold my congratulations. Now the only marring of our perfect joy is that your sore throat may prove to be more serious than you seem to anticipate. We rejoice with the most heartfelt joy that you have so bravely defended your country and escaped unharmed. Now I am satisfied that you have participated with honor in the greatest victory we will have during the war."

Lieutenant Elliott wrote James from San Francisco: "Everybody is delighted that you had so much success at Donelson, and I was right glad to get your letter about it. You have hosts of friends here, Mac. Miss Emily is in good health and spirits. She seems in much better spirit than she used to be, but every thought is about you, Mac, and she is very proud of you.

"I am sorry you didn't get Silmer at Donelson. I see he ran off with Floyd, a man he denounced every day of his life."

2. The Battle of Shiloh

In early March when McPherson returned from St. Louis, he brought instructions to General Grant for the movement up the

Tennessee River. As the rebels under General Albert S. Johnston were concentrating near Pittsburgh Landing, not far from Shiloh Church, it seemed certain that the next engagement would be fought near there.

McPherson did staff duty with exactness and gallantry. After reconnoitering the territory, he made specific remarks about the placement of troops, the most important being that they should not be deployed with their backs to the river. Unfortunately, when early on Sunday morning, April 6, the rebels attacked suddenly and vigorously. Grant's men were not more than a mile west of the river, and had not yet reached their assigned places.

It was practically a surprise attack, for which there seemed little excuse. General Grant who had established his headquarters at Savannah, nine miles from the army, had not yet appeared on the scene. The Union troops tried to hold their quickly allotted positions but were slowly forced back, and heavy fighting continued.

Many of the northern army were raw, untrained boys who had just acquired guns on the trip from Cairo and hardly knew how to load them. Some of these lads fled when the firing began; but most of the regiments held their lines in the face of repeated attacks, although they were pushed back almost to the river. Hundreds were killed or wounded. The rebels recklessly threw their troops into the battle until late afternoon when their general was killed. His loss was reflected in their diminishing efforts.

Dusk and the weary condition of the rebels saved the day for the North; both armies were exhausted. After dark General Buell and General Lew Wallace brought reinforcements for Grant, and all the men slept on the ground in a heavy rain. A newspaper correspondent described the terrible midnight scene —surgeons using the knife . . . no anesthetic . . . amputated arms and legs everywhere . . . men groaning with pain . . . blinding rain adding to their misery.

McPherson stayed on the field all night helping the wounded. He found that many of the Clyde boys in the 72d Ohio O.V.I. were casualties. As the injured were being taken from the bloody field to be placed on boats waiting to take them to hospitals in Cairo and Cincinnati, a man approached whom James at once recognized as Elijah Brownell, one of the friends of his youth in Stemtown. "Lige," he said. Lige had become a master mechanic and had been drafted by the government to keep engines repaired on boats plying the Mississippi and Tennessee rivers. Now he helped James until all the wounded had been placed on the boat. Then he and Lige raised their hands in farewell.

On the second day, fighting continued until late afternoon.

> General Grant, accompanied by Colonel McPherson and Major Hawkins, had been riding back and forth to see the progress made. They were moving along the northern edge of a clearing toward the river above the landing. No enemy appeared until suddenly a battery with musketry opened upon them from the edge of the wood. The shells and balls whistled about their ears very fast for a minute. It took them no longer to get out of sight.
>
> In the sudden start Major Hawkins lost his hat. McPherson's horse was panting as if ready to drop. On examination it was found that a ball had struck him forward of the flank just back of the saddle and had gone entirely through. In a few minutes the poor beast dropped dead. A ball had struck the metal scabbard of Grant's sword just below the hilt and broken it nearly off. All were thankful it was no worse.[2]

On the seventh the Rebels, with Beauregard as their leader, attacked, but Grant, with his reinforcements, pushed them back to Shiloh Church. Neither army seemed anxious to resume fighting, and they rested within six miles of each other.

Later the Rebels retreated toward Corinth. General Grant, in reporting to General Halleck on the battle of Shiloh wrote, "Col. McPherson, attached to my staff as Chief Engineer, deserves more than a passing notice for his activity and courage."

When the public learned of the appalling loss of life at Shiloh and of the seeming blunders that caused it, many were inclined to put the blame on General Grant. Halleck, who had not warmed up to Grant, decided after considering all the reports he received, that he would take command in person of all the forces now centered north of Corinth. McPherson was again assigned to his staff as Chief Engineer, while Grant was practically ignored. Halleck, "Old Brains" as he was called, was a man of excessive caution; he thought the roads to Corinth, because of the railroad junction, should be fortified. His knowledge of warfare was more theoretical than practical. He gave McPherson orders to prepare a line of parapets extending for miles, the making of which slowed the advance of the army at times to a rate of about a quarter of a mile a day. Most of the month of May was taken up by this project.

McPherson obeyed the orders though he considered the unusual delays needless; he thought it of more importance to advance quickly on the enemy's works. Halleck and his army of 100,000 men finally neared Corinth, which was occupied by the Confederates under Beauregard. After a few skirmishes the rebels quietly evacuated the town during the night of May 29, 1862, and Halleck's army took possession.

Halleck was summoned to Washington and was made General-in-Chief, where his peculiar talents could be used more fittingly than as a field officer. Grant was made Commander of the Department of Tennessee. He at once recommended that McPherson be promoted to a Brigadier-Generalship of Volunteers and Military Superintendent of Railroads. His request was complied with June 4, 1862.[3]

The victory at Shiloh gave the Union control of the Tennessee River south to the Memphis and Charleston Railroad. In June the city of Memphis fell to the bombardment of the river boats. Commander Farragut had but recently taken New Orleans, leaving Vicksburg the only city of importance on the Mississippi River in the hands of the Confederates. The land forces must now lay plans for the capture of that city.

James, having learned that Russell had resigned his position in Cincinnati, asked him to become auditor of the military railroads. He also asked him to procure in that city some clothes for his role as brigadier general.

He received the following reply from Russ:

> I could find nothing ready made that would suit you in the way of coat or pants and, supposing you were in something of a hurry, I had to order them from a firm which promised to have them ready to-morrow night. The flannel you will find is of pretty good quality but I will not answer for the workmanship. All our best tailors are so crowded with work that none of them would promise to have them before the last of next week. Of shoulders straps I know nothing. I ordered a pair at $8 which the dealer told me was of good quality and cheap.
>
> I shall be glad to accept your invitation to a military position, and I shall await your orders.

During the summer months James was kept busy repairing the railroads. As a brigadier general of volunteers and as a member of Grant's staff, he had to find the most strategic places to deploy the widespread army in order to protect Memphis, Corinth and other points that might be attacked. It was a time of waiting during which McPherson and his engineers prepared their plans for any eventuality, knowing that an attack would come from either Price or Van Doren.

> In early October Grant notified McPherson that telegraphic communication with Rosecrans at Corinth was cut. He assumed that the rebels were attacking, and he wished McPherson to conduct re-inforcements there at once. McPherson immediately mustered his

men from the railroads and with troops sent him by Grant, moved rapidly toward Corinth. As he neared the town the sounds of guns grew louder. Not knowing the position of the enemy, he threw skirmishers to the front and carefully advanced till he reached Rosecrans's pickets.

The rebels, seeing the fresh troops advancing, started to retreat and were followed closely by McPherson's men. In a short time a party of the rebels came back with a flag of truce and said their purpose was to care for the wounded and bury the dead. McPherson ordered it to stand aside. "Fighting is going on," said he, "and I do not propose to suspend it unless ordered to do so by the command General."

He attacked the enemy, captured a baggage train and a large quantity of materials, and dispatched the retreating army in disorderly flight.

It was McPherson's first handling of troops in action. He was left to his own judgment, and so fully did he show his ability that shortly after, he received another promotion. On his return from this pursuit, October 8, General Grant, who believed him capable of great things, gave him the news of his appointment as Major General.[4]

CHAPTER XVII

Major General James B. McPherson

On October 20, 1862, James wrote to his mother telling of his promotion:

Bolivar, Tenn.

MY DEAR MOTHER,

I have been so busy for the last few days that I have had but little time to write letters and I have trusted to Russ to keep you advised of my movements. Little did I think, my dear mother, when I saw you all last November, that I should ever be a Major General in the Army of the United States, but so it is.

My appointment was a perfect surprise, as I did not think I had earned it. As soon as it was announced, I was assigned to duty in command of this Post and came here four days ago. My appointment takes me away from the railroads, though Russ will still retain his position as Treasurer and Auditer if he wishes to. I prefer to have him remain for some time yet and not leave because I am assigned to other duty.

You have, of course, read all about the battles of Corinth and Dan's Ridge and the subsequent pursuit of the enemy as we followed him up sharply as far as Ripley, Miss. My Division had the advance all the way to Ripley, and skirmished a good deal with the enemy. We remained in Ripley two days and a half, and then marched back quietly, my Division constituting the rear guard.

My love to all at home,
Your Affec. Son,
JAMES

"On October 15th, 1862, one week after McPherson's promotion to the rank of Major General, the employees of the Military railroads of the Department of Tennessee, showed their admiration for him by presenting him with a horse, saddle, bridle and sword. About 8 o'clock in the evening 150 officers and employees of the railroads assembled in the parlors of the hotel in Jackson, Tenn. There were speeches of presentation and congratulations. The General, deeply moved, replied in a plain, courteous and unaffected manner."[1]

The following day McPherson proceeded to the headquarters assigned him. He organized and equipped his troops; had his scouts constantly watching the movements along the front; and gathered information that enabled Grant to plan his campaign against Holly Springs and thence to the rear of Vicksburg.

On November 11, McPherson was ordered to make a reconnoissance in force toward Holly Springs. When about ten miles south of Old Lamar, he encountered the enemy in force. He at once placed his infantry in front and pushed with the cavalry around the rebels' right flank. As the foot soldiers advanced in front, the cavalry attacked the rear. After a short resistance the enemy broke and fled in disorder. The result was more successful than had been expected.

"The sagacity and foresight displayed, his quickness in grasping the mistakes of his enemy, the speed of his attacks, his care of the lives of his men and his unrelenting pressure of the enemy's lines when broken, marked him in the minds of all who witnessed him at Lamar as an officer destined for high command."[2]

In the stress and turmoil of warfare, James found comfort and spiritual support in the messages he received from home and friends. Mrs. Robert Smith wrote him on November 24:

> I know it will give you pleasure to hear from home. I saw your mother and grandmother last week. Your grandmother was very smart indeed. She had just completed a quilt for a poor soldier's wife. She had done all the work herself. Her first words to me were, "Well, Jimmie has become a great man." My reply was, "He is no less good for being great." Of course I can sympathize with her in her pride. She is not the only one to rejoice over your good fortune. I can assure you it is a great satisfaction to see your name mentioned every week in the papers, and so honorably, too.
>
> Russell, I suppose, keeps you informed of all that is passing at home, so I will only say that I never saw your mother so really happy as when I was there last week. She had just received a very satisfactory letter from Russ.

A short time after McPherson's successful engagement at Lamar, Grant saw that it was time to move against Price into Mississippi. He entrusted to McPherson the advance of the Army of the Tennessee and the command of its entire left wing. This campaign continued through November and December and would have been successful but for the unnecessary surrender of the supply depots of the army at Holly Springs on December 20, 1862. All the supplies for this campaign being lost, the army was compelled to withdraw from Mississippi.

> On this return march, McPherson commanded the rear guard through all the exhausting march over the flooded country. They fell back stubbornly though harassed on all sides, while Grant's Army was moving with its trains, artillery and baggage. McPherson was in the saddle night and day; the rain fell in torrents; the roads were almost bottomless; the Army moved slowly,

yet he never became impatient, nor left a position until he saw the last wagon at a safe distance on its way. His troops cheerfully lived on quarter rations and patiently endured the fatigues when they saw their Commander asking no sacrifices of them that he did not make himself.[3]

CHAPTER XVIII

On to Vicksburg

In December, 1862, General Grant was authorized to divide his army into five corps as follows: Thirteenth Army Corps, Major General McClernand; the Fourteenth, Major General George H. Thomas; the Fifteenth, Major General W. T. Sherman; the Sixteenth, Major General Hurlburt; the Seventeenth, Major General James B. McPherson.

McPherson assumed command of the Seventeenth Corps in January, 1863, and immediately organized it into three divisions of infantry, with an artillery unit and a brigade of cavalry. He spent the rest of the month massing and reorganizing his troops at Memphis, Tennessee.

> On his way to Memphis, he occupied the rear car while the rest of the train was filled with the sick and wounded of his command. On a cold winter night, as the train was rounding a sharp curve, every car except the one in which McPherson rode, was thrown from the track and carried down a deep embankment. The wounded men were again badly injured. McPherson did everything in his power to help them; then leaving them in charge of his medical director, he climbed into

the locomotive which still remained on the track, and hurried forward to send back further relief.[1]

The following letter from McPherson was read to his troops:[2]

Memphis, Tenn., Feb. 10, 1863.

Officers and Soldiers of the 17th Army Corps,

Our marching orders have come, and it is for us to respond with promptness and alacrity. We move to capture the stronghold of the Rebels in the valley of the Mississippi. That our success is certain I have not the slightest doubt if you bring to the performance of the work the same zeal, ability and patriotic devotion to your country which have marked your course thus far.

I know that I do not speak to the heroes of Fort Donelson, Shiloh and Corinth in vain. The record of your past services, glorious as it is, is but a pledge of the future. We go forward to strike a blow against this most unjustifiable rebellion; we go to plant our flag upon the ramparts of Vicksburg. I know that I but echo your sentiments when I say that each and everyone of you desires to battle earnestly until this great work is accomplished.

By the twenty-second of February McPherson's troops were ready for the field; by the twenty-third, they began arriving at Lake Providence, Louisiana. That winter was noted for heavy rainfall and for continuous high water in the Mississippi River and its tributaries. Vicksburg was the first high land below Memphis, and everywhere else were lakes and swamps, which made it impossible to march directly against Vicksburg from the north, east of the Mississippi. There was no place where the army could stand and do battle against the city.

Grant saw that he must get the troops south of the city in order to attack. Several plans were tried to find a water passage far enough from the shore batteries for safety. Canals were dug in order to connect the waters of the bayous and allow passage, but they availed nothing.

McPherson was assigned to try to get through the sluggish waters of Lake Providence, Bayou Macon, and the Red River; it was almost a hopeless project, and McPherson gave no opinion as to its success; but he went to work to carry out his orders. After three weeks of futile experimenting it was given up. Several other attempts proved fruitless.

These efforts only provided mirth for the enemy, who jeered at the "Yankee ditch-diggers." Meantime, the news relayed to the North was that six different projects had failed to find a passage past Vicksburg. Northern newspapers were criticizing the inactivity of the army; were even urging that Grant be replaced by another commander. The case was becoming desperate.

Grant, who had a plan he had been speculating on for some time finally divulged it to his generals and to Commodore Porter. Grant decided to march his army southward on the Louisiana side; to cross the Mississippi below the last of the chain of rebel defenses; to march north on the east side of the river; to trust for supplies on the country and to the gunboats that might run the gauntlet of the Vicksburg batteries.

The plan received different responses. Sherman was aghast. "I am utterly opposed to it," he said. The others thought it worth trying; much better than rotting in the bayous.

It was an audacious scheme that meant either success or obliteration for Grant. With Sherman still opposing it, he put the plan into operation on the night of April 16. The rebels opened fire and houses were set ablaze for miles to illuminate the targets.

A more fantastic scene can hardly be imagined; the gunboats, some of them wrapped in cotton bales and looking like whited ghosts belching fire and smoke, answered the shore batteries, while blazing houses threw spectral lights and shadows on the pageant. Only one boat was lost and several were more or less damaged; the flotilla arrived at Bruinsburg, south of Vicksburg.

A few nights later other protected boats and barges, loaded with supplies, passed Vicksburg safely. By May 1 all of the troops were on the east bank of the river south of the city. They were given four days' rations and were expected to live off the country after that.

One of McPherson's divisions, under General John Logan,[3] immediately moved against Port Gibson and took an important part in the battle that scattered the enemy from their position. After their defeat, the rebels fled and burned the bridge over Bayou Pierre. Bringing up the rest of his troops, McPherson rebuilt the bridge, crossed in pursuit and continued the advance.

Overtaking the rebels at Raymond, he attacked unaided by the other corps and inflicted a disastrous defeat on the enemy. Just as the issue of the battle seemed determined, McPherson's adjutant general gave him a dispatch he had written to send to Grant and awaited McPherson's signature to it. The message read: "Have met the enemy in superior force, but have defeated him disastrously, and am now in full pursuit." McPherson quietly tore it up, then wrote in the adjutant's field-book: "We met the enemy about three today; have had a hard fight but up to this time have the advantage. Signed, J. B. Mc."

Next day he came upon the railroad station at Clinton and destroyed some cars and buildings.

In the meantime, General Joseph E. Johnston, divining the plan of the Federals to destroy him before concentrating on Vicksburg, ordered Pemberton to join him at once near Jackson to prevent such catastrophe. But Pemberton's only thought was to guard the city he commanded. He disobeyed the summons, thinking he could best save Vicksburg by remaining there with his troops.

During this time McPherson was continuing his race toward Jackson, which he reached at ten o'clock on the morning of May 14, after traveling through one of the most severe storms encountered during the entire campaign. He rested his men for a brief time, then led to the attack. The lines moved slowly at first, gradually increasing their speed, till finally they dashed forward with loud cheering. Johnston, disobeyed by his subordinate, on whose troops he had confidently counted, put up a fight that lasted for three hours. At the end of that time, the flag of the "Seventeenth" waved from the dome of the capitol of Mississippi, and General Joe Johnston's forces had retreated across the Pearl River. The battle of Jackson was fought by the Seventeenth Corps, though Sherman stood within supporting distance in event of disaster. That night Grant slept in the room occupied by Johnston the previous night.

Generals Grant, Sherman and McPherson met in the large Hotel in Jackson. Here the former explained that dispatches from General Pemberton to General Johnston had been intercepted showing they had planned to join their forces. The three generals decided quickly how to prevent such a union. McPherson was ordered to march back early the next day on the Clinton road to join McClernand; Sherman was ordered to remain one day to break up railroads, and to destroy the arsenal, factories and anything that would be of help to the enemy; then to follow McPherson.

Before daylight McPherson was on the march, facing Vicksburg. The next day, May 16, he met Pemberton, who was trying to obey Johnston's order to join him. But his tardy obedience came too late, for his line of march lay across McPherson's front on Champion Hill, where a bloody battle was fought during the day. Hovey's division was the only assistance given McPherson's men, although McClernand's corps had been ordered to fight. When Logan's division threatened the enemy's rear, the rebels fled. Two thousand prisoners were taken but only at the cost of two thousand killed and wounded.

McPherson advanced to the Big Black River and built two bridges, one of them a floating bridge laid on cotton bales. Crossing these, he quickly came to the fortifications of Vicksburg, where he deployed his troops. He held the center across the Jackson–Vicksburg road, opposed to the strongest works of the enemy. Sherman had the right and McClernand the left.

Pemberton, who in his hour of indecision had wavered between flight from the enemy and a last-ditch defense of Vicksburg, at last shut himself in the city, thus sealing his fate. Grant made two assaults on the Confederate position but both were repulsed, so he settled down to a siege. Sappers and miners began digging saps and trenches under the rebel forts.

McPherson directed the placing of the big guns that in a few days were sweeping the enemy's defenses on both flanks. His sharpshooters picked off so many rebels that their artillery became silent at times. Night and day shells were being thrown into the city constantly by gunboats on the river and by Grant's siege guns. To escape them, the inhabitants dug caves in the high bluff and lived in them during the siege. Food was very scarce in the city and soldiers and civilians were hungry. Many people tried to escape but few succeeded. The weather was hot and sanitary conditions were bad.

McPherson gave orders to his engineers to construct a mine under Fort Hill, this being the first experiment of its kind attempted in the war. By June 24th, his Chief Engineer Captain Hickenlooper, reported that the mine was ready; that twenty-two hundred pounds of powder had been placed there and in the saps leading to it. McPherson told Grant that the explosion would take place at three o'clock on the afternoon of June 25th. Just before that hour, thousands of men in blue had filed into the entrenchments, supplies of ammunition were rushed in; the artillery was primed for a grand assault; one hundred picked men were placed to storm into the breach; a death-like silence was on everything. A few minutes before three, Grant and Sherman came to watch the result with McPherson of this new instrument of destruction.

At three o'clock a match was lighted to the fuse. In a few moments the rebel fort before them rose into the air a hundred feet. It began to break into fragments and finally seemed to disappear, leaving only a great cloud of black smoke. Through this roared thousands of muskets and the great guns along miles of entrenchments. The storming column of a hundred men dashed forward followed by their supports. They fought hand to hand for some time. Finally artillery was so placed as to secure the ground they had won. The result was not conclusive, however, because the amount of explosive was insufficient.[4]

McPherson ordered another mine under that part of Fort Hill still remaining. On the first of July this was exploded with great success. The fort was demolished. Several of the garrison were thrown within the Federal lines. The success of these operations gave the Union army possession of the key to the Vicksburg area.

Pemberton, who realized the hopelessness of his situation and the destitution of his people, concluded he could no longer hold the city. On July 2 he sent a note to Grant asking for an armistice to consider terms of surrender. On July 3 General Grant sent word to Pemberton that an interview would be granted him on McPherson's front. Pemberton appointed 3 P.M., July third.

Grant was there with his staff and with Generals Ord, McPherson, Logan and A. J. Smith. Pemberton came late, attended by General Bowen and Colonel L. M. Montgomery. Grant heard what the rebels had to say and left them at the end of an hour and a half, saying he would send them his ultimatum in writing before evening, to which Pemberton promised to reply before night; hostilities were to cease in the meantime.

Grant then conferred at his headquarters with his corps and division commanders. All of them, except Steele, favored a plan proposed by McPherson and which Grant finally adopted. The main features of the plan were unconditional surrender, the garrison to be treated as prisoners of war, then later paroled. At 6 P.M. Grant sent the terms to Pemberton, who immediately wrote accepting them with a few minor changes to which Grant consented. General Grant told McPherson that his Seventeenth Corps would have the honor of being first to enter the city.

At 10 A.M., July 4, 1863, white flags appeared along the entire Confederate lines, and immediately after, the Confederate army marched outside their entrenchments with their colors flying. They formed line, stacked their arms, laid their colors on the stacks, about faced and marched back within their entrenchments as prisoners of war.

McPherson's corps immediately followed, led by Major General Grant and his staff. Into the heart of shell-torn Vicksburg they marched with colors flying and bands playing. The citizens ventured out of the caves in which they had been living to see the spectacle.

When the procession had climbed the hill to the courthouse, it halted. A unit of McPherson's command climbed up the steep steps leading to the building, and in a short time the Stars and Stripes was placed on the cupola of the great old colonnaded landmark.

The next day unarmed boats traveled past Vicksburg. Upon hearing of the city's capitulation, President Lincoln remarked, "The Father of waters again goes unvexed to the sea."

In the military operations thus ended, General McPherson had shown the leading qualifications of a corps general. He had been skillful and judicious when left to his own resources; he had shown discretion in handling his troops; many of his engineering devices were new to warfare and had a startling effect upon the country. He was the youngest of the corps generals and the least experienced. Now he was compared to Sherman and even to Grant, sometimes to their disadvantage. In the two months' campaign, McPherson had thus risen to rank beside the most highly regarded commanders in the Federal armies.

At the time of this campaign, Grant's ability as a leader was not well known. It was in the later war years that his great generalship was demonstrated. The execution of the plans to the rear of Vicksburg was so brilliant that people refused to give him credit for it. In deciding who the genius was that inspired him, both North and South insisted it must be McPherson, his staff officer whom he had made one of his corps commanders. It shows the impression that the abilities of McPherson had made upon the general public.

General Grant himself was most generous in giving praise to the gifted McPherson. Shortly after the surrender, he prepared two letters for the War Department. One told of the services and merits of Sherman; the other of McPherson, recommending each for promotion to brigadier generalship in the regular army. The language of Grant's letter concerning McPherson was just and magnanimous:

> He has been with me in every battle since the commencement of the rebellion except Belmont. At Henry, Donelson, Pittsburg Landing and the siege of Corinth,

as a staff officer and engineer his services were conspicuous and highly meritorious. At the second battle of Corinth, his skill as a soldier was displayed in successfully carrying re-inforcements to the besieged garrison when the enemy was between him and the point to be reached.

In the advance through central Mississippi, General McPherson commanded one wing of the army with all the ability possible to show, he having the lead in the advance and the rear in retiring.

In the campaign and siege terminating in the fall of Vicksburg, General McPherson has borne a conspicuous part. At the battle of Fort Gibson it was under his direction that the enemy was driven late in the afternoon from a position they had succeeded in holding all day against an obstinate attack. His Corps, the advance, always under his immediate eye, were the pioneers in the movement from Fort Gibson to Hankinson's Ferry.

From the North Fork of the Bayou Pierre to Black River it was a constant skirmish, the whole skillfully managed. The enemy was so closely pressed as to be unable to destroy their bridge of boats after them. From Hankinson's Ferry to Jackson, McPherson's Corps, the Seventeenth, marched roads not traveled by other troops, fighting the entire battle of Raymond alone; and the bulk of Johnston's army was fought by this Corps entirely under the management of General McPherson. At Champion Hills, the Seventeenth Army Corps and General McPherson were conspicuous. All that could be termed a battle there was fought by General McPherson's Corps and General Hovey's division of the Thirteenth Corps. In the assault of the 23rd of May on the fortifications of Vicksburg and during the entire siege, General McPherson and his command took unfading laurels.

He is one of the ablest engineers and most skillful Generals. I would respectfully but urgently recommend his promotion to the position of Brigadier General in the regular army.

The nomination was promptly made. The confirmation was for a while a little uncertain. McPherson's administration of the regulations established in Vicksburg were of such a humane character that some northern people, even northern newspapers, accused him of undue sympathy for the rebels. An officer of high rank, who had been one of his teachers at West Point, told McPherson about this unjust accusation. The latter was angry but replied, "I have done nothing to justify the suspicions of rebel sympathy, save what the dictates of humanity suggest. When the time comes that to be a soldier a man has to overlook the claims of humanity, then I do not want to be a soldier."[5]

In due time the confirmation was easily secured. In the meantime another distinction was conferred upon him. It was the Gold Medal of Honor awarded by the Board of Honor, composed of fellow soldiers in Grant's army, in testimony of the appreciation in which he and his work were held by those who knew him best.

In the midst of his pressing business, James found time to write to Robert Smith:[6]

Vicksburg, July 21, 1863.

DEAR ROBERT,

I have been intending ever since our entry into this place to write you a long letter, as well as one to Kate and Clemmy in whose debt I am in very largely. But the surrender of Vicksburg brought with it very little rest for me. I was immediately placed in command of all the forces, and charged with paroling the prisoners and carrying out the terms of capitulation. I tell you, Robert, it was a glorious "Fourth of July" for us down here, and though we did not have much time to celebrate it in the approved style, we enjoyed it immensely.

About 11 A.M. the "Old Flag" was hoisted on the Court House and, as our soldiers marched past coming

> in to the take possession of the City and defenses, each Regiment gave three rousing cheers for the Flag.
>
> I would like above all things to run up home and see you all, but I cannot get away. A great many officers want to go and, as most of them have families and important private business to attend to, their claims are more urgent than mine and they must go first.

Perhaps the greatest value to the North of the capture of Vicksburg was its cutting the Confederacy in two. It also set the armies used in its conquest free for other purposes. On the day of its capitulation the great battle of Gettysburg was won. Those two decisive victories for the North, occurring at the same time, should have ended the war. But the rebel leaders and politicians worked upon the natural pride of the southern people, trying to make them believe they would eventually win; many southerners fought on, knowing in their hearts they could not succeed. Many soldiers deserted and thousands of boys were killed or wounded needlessly in ensuing battles.

After the fall of Vicksburg, McPherson's corps remained in and near the city. Grant's troops were dispersed in outlying sections of the surrounding territory; Sherman's men encamped along the Black River. Grant and Sherman had their families with them, and each of the three generals occupied a house in Vicksburg.

These three Ohio men were West Point men; they were great soldiers; they were unquestionably the greatest leaders of the Federal army. They were congenial and frank, and they openly discussed every idea, every plan, every possibility that each one had in his mind concerning the war.

Other officers had their wives with them in Vicksburg during the late summer and fall of 1863. There were many picnics and social affairs, many of them attended by the citizens, with whom McPherson had become popular. Even the Yankee-hating belles of Vicksburg concluded he was as polite as a southern gentleman, and therefore worthy of their attention, and even of a little admiration.

CHAPTER XIX

War Postpones the Wedding

1. Commander McPherson

General McPherson was made commander of the Vicksburg area and immediately took charge of the city. He appointed many committees to put things in order and restore living conditions. He ordered General Logan to appoint three persons, one a commissioned officer, one a chaplain to be selected from his command, and one citizen of reliable character, to constitute a committee to visit the citizens of the town, to point out the most needy and destitute persons and issue them provisions.

Negroes were allowed to go with officers if they wanted to, but there must be no coercion.

All Confederate flags collected were to be sent to Washington. Paroling of prisoners and other work was not accomplished until the middle of July.

McPherson ordered Brigadier General F. G. Ransom, commander of United States forces in Natchez to "collect all the cattle, arms, ammunition, lumber and stores of all kinds that will be of advantage to us. Send by boats properly convoyed to Vicksburg."

Regardless of his many responsibilities, James never failed to take time out to write his daily letter to his sweetheart in faraway San Francisco. Two long years had passed since they had parted, each fondly hoping he would soon return. Now, there was good news! James received a letter from his friend Lieutenant Elliott saying:

> MY DEAR MAC,
> I just received your Vicksburg letter and hasten to congratulate you. All accounts of the surrender were received here with wild joy and pride. You have no idea, Mac, of San Francisco's pride in you. Even your Southern friends here are converted to your views, especially since the papers are carrying stories of your humane treatment of the people of Vicksburg. But we who know you knew it would not be otherwise. Several of them have talked to me about the futility of the Confederates continuing the war. It is a shame, for the South will undoubtedly suffer for it. . . . Nellie and I called on the McLanes Friday evening. Miss Emily was busy preparing for her trip east. I never saw her look so well nor appear so happy. You know, dear Mac, my wishes for you both.

The exact date of Emily Hoffman's return to Baltimore is not known, but letters show that it was in the fall of 1863. She and James planned to be married as soon as he could properly leave his many duties. A large territory embracing the region bordering the Mississippi from Helena, Arkansas, to the mouth of the Red River, had been added to the area he already commanded. This greatly increased his responsibilities, making the time for his furlough vastly more uncertain. But the distance separating James from his sweetheart was lessened considerably, and the future assumed a brighter tinge for them.

The bitterness that Emily's mother had felt toward James had softened, for he had shown his caliber in two years of warfare. He was now proclaimed one of the nation's great men. His rise to success and fame was unprecedented. Emily's niece said, "Her mother had consented to the marriage, and Aunt Emily returned to Baltimore bringing her trousseau with her."[1]

James, longing to see his Emily, discussed the situation with Grant, hoping that some way might be found for him to visit her in Baltimore. But he knew only too well that affairs were such as to preclude his making the trip for some unpredictable time.

About the first of March, the War Department issued orders giving a thirty-day furlough to all enlisted soldiers whose time of enlistment was up and who would re-enlist for the duration. That order, which depleted the army's strength, was criticized by Sherman and other officers. However, they saw the necessity of it, as most of the soldiers, particularly of McPherson's corps, had served for two full years. McPherson, therefore, made an earnest effort to secure the re-enlistment of his men. In this he was highly successful, thanks to the confidence the men had in him. Later he was able to report to the Secretary of War that his entire command would re-enlist after the thirty-day furlough. It was said that no other corps general in the country could equal that report.

But the furlough promised McPherson's men was delayed for a time. He explained to them that the enemy was active in northern Mississippi, making raids in the Vicksburg area; that it was necessary to dispatch troops there at once, because of the great amount of war material stored at Meridian. An expedition under General Sherman was organized to destroy the stores. This consisted of the Sixteenth and Seventeenth Army Corps under Generals Hurlburt and McPherson. They marched straight to Meridian, which they reached on the fourteenth of February. They destroyed an arsenal and storehouses, and broke up sixty miles of railroad.

The rebel forces throughout the state were now without supplies, and they were so demoralized that further raids were no longer feared. Sherman felt safe in taking men away from Vicksburg for the spring campaign in the east, and he left at once for Chattanooga.

While still in Vicksburg, Grant, Sherman and McPherson had been making plans for that area. Early in March Sherman wrote to McPherson concerning troop movements to reinforce the army at Chattanooga. He explained: "I want you to push matters as rapidly as possible, and to do all you can to put two handsome divisions of your own Corps at Cairo, ready to embark up the Tennessee River by the 20th or 30th of April at the very furthest. I wish it could be done sooner, but the promise of these thirty days furlough, though politic, is very unmilitary. It deprives us of our ability to calculate as to time; but do the best you can.

"Steal a furlough and run to Baltimore, but get back in time to take part in the next grand move."[2]

General Grant was ordered east in March, 1864, to command all the armies of the United States, and personally, the Army of the Potomac. He wrote the following to General Sherman, expressing his feelings to both Sherman and McPherson:[3]

> The bill reviving the grade of Lieutenant General in the Army has become a law, and my name has been sent to the Senate for the place. . . .
>
> While I have been eminently successful in this war, in at least gaining the confidence of the public, no one feels more than I how much of the success is due to the energy, skill and the harmonious putting forth of that energy and skill of those whom it has been my good fortune to have occupying subordinate positions under me.
>
> But what I want is to express my thanks to you and McPherson as the men to whom, above all others, I feel indebted for whatever I have had of success. How far your advice and suggestions have been of assistance, you know. How far your execution of whatever has been given to you to do, entitles you to the reward I am receiving, you cannot know as well as I do. I feel all the gratitude this letter would express, giving it the most flattering construction.
>
> The word YOU, I use in the plural, intending it for McPherson, also, and I shall so write him.
>
> U. S. GRANT, MAJOR GENERAL

When Grant left his western army for his eastern career, Sherman was appointed to succeed him. McPherson received the command of Sherman's Army of the Tennessee.

"Of these two lieutenants of the rarest powers," said Colonel Chesney of the British Royal Engineers, "it is hard to say whether Grant leaned more on the calm courage and unfailing resources of Sherman, or upon the subtle genius and daring spirit of McPherson, a soldier of the very highest promise."[4]

The following is one of the many newspaper comments on Grant's elevation:[5]

> Mr. Lincoln's order appointing Lieut. General Grant to the command of all the armies in the field and naming as his subordinates Halleck, Sherman, and McPherson, is a curious commentary upon the reliability of the estimate which the daily press and the public is likely to put upon our military men. [This refers to the criticisms leveled at Grant and Sherman earlier in the war.]
>
> General McPherson, fortunately for himself, has thus far managed to escape hostile criticism; but the Rebels have given their testimony of his ability, and General Grant takes so much pride in rewarding those who have assisted him in achieving his greatest successes, that he has promptly advanced this officer to the position which he believes his brilliant talents qualify him to fill.

2. James Has a Furlough

McPherson left Vicksburg on March 26, 1864, for a twenty-day furlough. He started north by boat to Cairo, intending to pay a short visit to his people in Clyde, then to proceed to Baltimore, where his long-deferred marriage to Emily Hoffman was to take place.

Because of war conditions and the short time allowed him, the wedding was to be a very quiet affair. Emily and her mother were to make all plans so that no time should be lost after he arrived. James and Emily had not seen each other since he had left California in August, 1861. The long years of waiting were ended and it appeared now that all the longings, the hopes and disappointments of that interval were to culminate in blissful reunion and wedlock.

James, like an eager boy, thought the boat traveled very slowly. He sent a telegram to Emily from every town where the boat stopped, apprising her of his progress toward her. She, as eagerly, found those places on her map—a map that had told her his approximate location each day since he had left her. The beautiful wedding garments she had brought from San Francisco were carefully inspected, and everything was made ready for the day of days.

When McPherson arrived in Cairo, he found two telegrams awaiting him. One told of his promotion: the other ordered him to proceed at once to Huntsville, Alabama, to help plan for the spring drive against Atlanta. He was stunned. Then a feeling of bitterness swept over him for a moment. He gave no thought to his promotion; only to the fact that the cup of happiness of which he was about to taste had been snatched away from him. "What will Emily think?" was the burden of his thoughts as, for the first time in his life, he was unable to solve his problem quickly. He must, of course, obey the order of his superior officer, although for the first time he felt a distaste for doing so. He would send a telegram to Emily. How cold that would be. She would be hurt, he knew, and James had never hurt any creature intentionally. It was almost more than he could bear; but he was a well-disciplined officer. He squared his shoulders and faced the inevitable.

He engaged a room in a hotel where he could sit quietly and try to think. He spent some time in composing a message to his sweetheart, after which he prepared to take the first boat to Huntsville. He would spend the time in writing her a letter.

By the time McPherson had reached Huntsville, advance units of his command at Vicksburg under Generals Logan and Blair were already on the move. They were enlarged daily by return of the men whose furloughs had expired.

General Sherman, whose four departments were commanded

by Major Generals Schofield, Ohio; Thomas, Cumberland; McPherson, Tennessee; and Steele, Arkansas, started to inspect his troops. McPherson, who had just arrived from Cairo, accompanied him on his tour of inspection, at the end of which the army commanders met in Chattanooga. There they talked freely and without reserve of matters then in progress or impending.

They knew that as soon as spring was open, they would have to move against the Confederates under General Joseph E. Johnston, who was securely entrenched at Dalton, thirty miles to the south.

Sherman instructed each commander to prepare immediately for a hard campaign. The most important question was getting sufficient supplies to the army, for the terrain was mountainous and there was but one railroad.

While plans for the campaign were being formulated, Emily was suffering keen disappointment because of the postponement of her wedding day and the continued absence of her lover. Though greatly pressed for time, General Sherman wrote the following to her, no doubt at the behest of McPherson, explaining the situation:[6]

> MY DEAR YOUNG LADY,
>
> It has come to my knowledge that you are affianced to a close friend and associate of mine, Major General McPherson, and from that, weighing mighty matters of state but lightly in the realms of love, you feel that he gives too much of his time to his country and too little to you.
>
> His rise in his profession has been rapid, steady and well earned. Each step in his progress, however, has imposed on him fresh duties that, as a man and a soldier, and still more as a patriot, he could not avoid. I did hope, as we returned from Meridian when his Corps was entitled to go home on furlough, that he, too, could steal a month to obey the promptings of his heart; to hasten to Baltimore and I so instructed; but by the changes incident to General Grant's elevation, McPher-

son succeeded to the command of a separate Army and Department, and could not leave. . . .

Would you have us leave our posts at the rudder of a ship in the midst of the angry sea of war? What would you think of the Captain of a California steamer who, regardless of the hundreds of human beings consigned to his care, would leave his deck to dally with his loved one below?

But I will not discuss so plain a point with one who bears the honored name of Hoffman; rather tell you of him so young but so prominent, whose corner is among the gallant and brave, who fights not for oppression and wrong, but that the government bequeathed to us by our ancestors shall not perish in ignominy and insult; but which shall survive in honor and glory, with a power to protect the weak and shelter the helpless from the terrible disasters of a patricidal war. . . .

I know McPherson well, as a young man and as a handsome and noble soldier, actuated by motives as pure as those of Washington. And I know that in giving my testimony to his high and noble character, I will not offend the girl he loves. Be patient, and I know that when the happy day comes for him to stand by your side, identical in heart and human existence, you will regard him with a high respect and honor that will convert simple love into something sublime and beautiful.

With great respect, I am
Your obedient servant,
W. T. Sherman

CHAPTER XX

On to Atlanta

The month of April, 1864, was taken up by Sherman and his generals in assembling their armies, procuring supplies, and discussing the routes to be followed. McPherson's absent divisions were collecting at Cairo and were gradually added to his command which, by the end of April, had left Huntsville for Chattanooga. Sherman's headquarters had been moved to the latter place from Nashville, and the three great armies of Thomas, Schofield and McPherson were sending advance troops from there to prearranged locales; Thomas to Ringgold, Schofield to Red Clay, and McPherson to Gordon's Mills. The two former generals were to advance to Dalton, and McPherson was to proceed to Resaca via Snake Creek Gap.

McPherson had the following letter read to his troops on May 5, 1864:

> Soldiers of the Army of the Tennessee,
>
> The successful issue of the battle may depend on your individual bravery, or the stubbornness which you hold your position. Be careful of your ammunition. Reserve your fire until the enemy is within effective range, then deliver it with deadly force, taking care to keep

cool and aim low. Should the enemy advance against you in line of battle with charged bayonets, do not wait quietly and receive the charge, but fix bayonets and receive him half way.

If any of your comrades fall wounded, do not leave the ranks to take them to the rear; an ample corps of men with stretchers and ambulances will follow close behind you to pick up the wounded. Press forward and gain the victory. Many a regiment on the battle-field has been sadly reduced in numbers to take the wounded to the rear.

Obey cheerfully and promptly the commands of your officers and rely implicitly on their judgment and discretion.

JAS. B. MCPHERSON
MAJOR GEN.

On May 5 began the great movement south. On the same day Grant began his movement against Lee. Sherman's plan to force Johnston out of his stronghold at Dalton was to keep him occupied with a strong army on his front, while another force moving south on his west flank should attack the railroad in his rear.[1] Then Johnston would move south to avoid this new danger, while the army on his front should follow after him, thus placing him between the two attacking forces.

In Sherman's plan, Thomas with 60,000 men was to make the feint on Johnston's front while McPherson with but 24,000 men was to make the flanking assault. Thomas, who knew that McPherson's forces were too few to carry out Sherman's plan, asked to advance on Resaca, but was not given permission to do so.

McPherson moved at once to carry out his orders. With the head of his column that had been given only enough rations for one day's march, he pushed on to Snake Creek Gap, below and west of Johnston's position. Here he met a force of rebel infantry. He attacked them, drove them off, and marched on toward Resaca. He soon learned that the cautious Johnston had anticipated such a move and had cut a road through the woods north to Dalton, by which any force marching on Resaca from the west could be attacked. He discovered that other roads led directly to Dalton. His spies now reached him with word that Johnston with 60,000 troops had evacuated Dalton and was marching by these roads upon this isolated force of 24,000.

McPherson saw that success lay in the speed with which his movements could be made. He ordered General Dodge to attack Resaca at once; while with the Fifteenth Corps he guarded this column against the threatened attack.

The movement seemed slowed up for some unknown reason. McPherson waited impatiently, then sent a staff officer to hasten it. The officer found General Sweeny, who commanded Dodge's advance, scolding some prisoners for taking up arms against the government. The officer explained the necessity of immediate movement, and gave him McPherson's orders. Sweeny said that his men were reforming and would move in a few minutes. A quarter of an hour passed. Again the staff officer urged speed; but still the troops did not move. The officer galloped back and reported the situation to McPherson. In a few minutes, McPherson came dashing to the front, and at once started the column. He told General Dodge the necessity for immediate assault, then returned to the Fifteenth Corps to await the attack.

But McPherson was contending against great odds: the poorly devised plan that had been made for him; the slow movements of subordinates; and his lack of cavalry. Dodge at last moved forward but, as a staff officer described it, "with little spirit, making but a weak attack, then returning to McPherson and reporting that the position could not be carried; that the enemy had more troops outside of their works than he had in his division." It appears that the subordinate officers were aware of the weakness of Sherman's plan, and were sure of disaster if it were executed.

It was now too late in the afternoon to make further maneuvers. The army was in danger of attack from Dalton, and could not go forward because of this failure before Resaca. There was nothing to do but go backward. McPherson, therefore, ordered the troops back three miles to the gap, where they strengthened their position, while he sent word of the result to Sherman.

The latter, who had received McPherson's first note at two o'clock stating that they had reached Resaca, was greatly disappointed upon receiving the second report. Sherman said:[2]

> McPherson had startled Johnston in his fancied security, but had not done the full measure of his work. He had 24,000 of the best men in the army and could have walked into Resaca, then held only by a small brigade, or he could have placed his whole force astride the railroad above Resaca and there have easily withstood the attack of all of Johnston's army, with the knowledge that Thomas and Schofield were at his heels. Had he done so, I am certain that Johnston would not have ventured to attack him in position but would have retreated eastward by Spring Place, and we should have captured half his army and all his artillery and wagons at the very beginning of the campaign.
>
> Such an opportunity does not occur twice in a single life but at the critical moment, McPherson seems to have been a little too cautious. Still he was perfectly justified at his orders.

McPherson had not startled Johnston. The fighting at Snake Creek Gap had revealed to Johnston the presence of McPherson's forces.

John Fiske sums up the situation: "For the purpose that Sherman had in view, McPherson's force was much too small. Sherman's mistake lay in not following Thomas's advice and sending Thomas himself with his 60,000 men through Snake Creek Gap instead of McPherson."[3]

Whitelaw Reid, war correspondent with the Army of the Tennessee, reported: "The initial fault of the movement lay, not in McPherson's caution, but in Sherman's plan of making the feint with the bulk of his army, and committing to this small column the burden of the real attack."[4]

Later Whitelaw Reid wrote, "It was a characteristic of Sherman's mind to be unwilling ever to acknowledge an error."[5]

Sherman must have seen his error, for the next day he sent Thomas's army to help McPherson oppose Johnston at Resaca.

Regardless of the best criticisms broached on this matter, Sherman did not change his opinion. In his *Memoirs,* published eleven years later, he used the same critical language he uttered on May 9, 1864, proving in this case at least that he did not acknowledge an error.

McPherson dispatched the following to Sherman:[6]

Camp at Sugar Valley, May 9th, 1864. 10:30 P.M.

The enemy has a strong position at Resaca naturally and, as far as we can see, has it well fortified. They displayed considerable force and opened on us with artillery. After skirmishing till after dark and finding that I could not succeed in cutting the railroad before dark or getting to it, I decided to withdraw the command and take up a position for the night between Sugar Valley and the entrance to the Gap for the following reasons:

1st. Between this point and Resaca there are a half dozen good roads leading north to Dalton down which a column of the enemy could march, making our advanced position a very exposed one.

2. General Dodge's men are all out of provisions, and some regiments have had nothing to-day. His wagon train is between here and Villanow and possibly some of them are passing through the Gap now, but they could not have reached near Resaca. Besides, I did not want to block the road with a train. It is very narrow and the country on either side is heavily wooded. I have no cavalry to feel out the flanks. If I could have had a division of good cavalry, I could have broken the railroad at some point.

I shall be compelled to rest my men to-morrow forenoon, at least, to enable them to draw provisions. When

> I move forward again I would like a division of Hooker's men to hold the entrance to the Gap and the roads at Sugar Valley, thereby enabling me to move forward with my entire command, except train guards.

The next day McPherson, reinforced by Thomas's Army, marched on to Resaca. Dalton fell at once, and Johnston hastened to Resaca to throw his entire force against the armies threatening his flank. The battle of Resaca followed. McPherson advanced against the center of the enemy's position and pushed a rebel corps before him. In spite of repeated attempts of the enemy to regain this advantage, McPherson stubbornly held fast to it. He sent Sweeny's division several miles further south to lay a pontoon bridge across the river and break the railroad in Johnston's rear. This was done and once more the rebel commander was forced to withdraw.

McPherson learned of Johnston's withdrawal immediately and at once followed up the retreating rebels. He ordered a heavy artillery fire, under which he advanced and destroyed one of the bridges over the Oostenaula; then he hastened south to the pontoon bridge he had ordered built. He struck the enemy's rear at Calhoun. He was resisted by the rebels long enough for them to get their trains away safely. But McPherson gave them no rest. He attacked them repeatedly and they repeatedly withdrew, until at Kingston he was forced to halt for supplies, which arrived in a short time. Then turning westward in order to avoid Allatoona Pass, he drew near Pumpkinvine Creek, where, on May 25, he again attacked the enemy.

While advanced units were skirmishing, he could hear several miles to the northeast the big guns of Thomas's army, which told him of heavy fighting in that quarter. He sped up his drive for some distance, then sent his cavalry in an effort to reach Thomas. Johnston seemed to sense McPherson's strategy and sent a strong force that compelled the cavalry to retreat. Because of his anxiety to communicate with Thomas and also with Sherman, he decided to send a staff officer with an escort. He relayed his plans for the next day to this officer, cautioning him to be sure, in some way, to find Sherman.

After dark the officer started and by midnight had reached Sherman. By morning he was back with news of Sherman's advance and the battle of New Hope Church; also with instructions to attack the enemy at Dallas.

By the time the messenger had returned, McPherson had already attacked the enemy and had driven him through Dallas and a mile beyond. But at that point, he was brought up against a fortified position that Johnston had prepared for an attack against his adversary. Next day the rebels attacked but McPherson stopped their charge and forced them back to other strong positions.

In the meantime, Sherman was meeting with checking movements wherever he tried to advance, Johnston facing him step by step till finally they confronted each other at Kenesaw Mountain, where the rebel general had strong entrenchments prepared. McPherson began his share of the attack on Kenesaw on the twenty-eighth of May.

Suddenly he was violently attacked on front and right. But his army was prepared for such an assault, for McPherson, with his usual regard for the lives of his men, had covered his front with breastworks so that his loss was comparatively small. The fighting before Kenesaw continued for a month with constant though not always severe attacks. The mountain appeared to be almost impregnable.

On June 3 McPherson received a letter from Russell, who had been on an extended furlough from his work on the military railroads. Written in Clyde, the letter said:

> I have inspected the sights of Nashville; I have trod the ante-diluvian sidewalks of Louisville; I have partaken of the contents of the fleshpots of New Orleans, and now, as did the prodigal son in the year ? B.C. (What year was it, Jim?), I have returned to my ancestral hearth where I have been welcomed in no small manner. (No fatted calf—just a nice fat hen.)
>
> My welcome, by the way, by my own flesh and blood as well as by the citizens, distinguished and otherwise, of this sequestered village, seems to be in exact

> ratio to my willingness to dilate upon the work, conversation, ability and accomplishments of a certain Major General James B. McPherson. When I confine my conversation to that subject, all the ears in Clyde stand up; when I digress, said ears flap down. . . .
>
> I have been here long enough to feel dissatisfied with myself. As long as this war is with us, I'll feel as if I should have some part in it. This place is too far away from you to afford me ordinary comfort. I can't live in the war zone and I can't live out of it. What the devil am I going to do?

James replied: "Perhaps you'd better return. I can't promise you comfort, but I'll guarantee some excitement. Memphis might be a neutral zone."

On June 4 McPherson received the last two divisions of the Seventeenth Corps returned from veteran furlough and one brigade of cavalry. These barely made up his losses sustained thus far in the campaign. These with new regiments brought the aggregate armies to their original strength.

On the twenty-seventh of June the whole combined army made a final assault on Kenesaw. McPherson's troops went directly up the mountain and were met with a withering fire. The Federal dead lay up against the Confederate breastworks. The assault failed. "Failure it was," said Sherman, "for which I accept the full responsibility." Sherman, seeing the futility of attacking entrenched lines, resumed his flanking movements the last of June.

McPherson withdrew from Kenesaw on the night of July 2 and tried a flanking movement on the rebels' right. Johnston discovered the movement and fell back, thus allowing McPherson to occupy Marietta. McPherson's advance now used all possible speed to prevent Johnston's crossing the Chattahoochee. Here, as in every place of strategical importance, the brilliant Johnston had prepared for all emergencies. He had built a strong bridgehead against which McPherson's forces fought without avail.

Since the opening of this campaign, these two most brilliant and resourceful generals had played a military chess game, each one anticipating the other's movements and slyly circumventing them. Here again, McPherson's cunning was displayed. By feinting with his cavalry to the southwest along the Chattahoochee, he attracted the attention of the enemy, who sent troops to occupy him should he force a crossing. He was thus enabled to move his army rapidly to the left till he reached Rosswell. Here he laid pontoons and also rebuilt the bridge, then crossed to the south side of the river. While he was crossing, other bridges and ferries were repaired, and soon the entire army had crossed the Chattahoochee.

CHAPTER XXI

Death of a Hero

1. Atlanta

On the seventeenth of July began the general movement against Atlanta, Thomas facing Peachtree Creek and Schofield on his left. McPherson neared the railroad leading to Decatur, which he reached that afternoon. There he turned toward Atlanta, breaking up the railroad as he advanced. On that same day, the southern army received a new commander in answer to appeals of the citizens of the city for a fighting general. The South, not realizing the importance of Johnston's bringing his army intact to Atlanta, had become dissatisfied with his retreating tactics and demanded his removal.

He was replaced by General John B. Hood, who had been a roommate of McPherson at West Point. Hood was forced to fight because the South wanted action. He was a brave man, but rash and naturally aggressive.

His first engagement as the new rebel commander was north of Atlanta, where he tried to carry out Johnston's plans against Thomas and Schofield at Peachtree Creek as they emerged from the swampy ground.[1] Here on the twentieth of July he was defeated. He retired to Atlanta, apparently giving up the territory to his adversaries.

Meanwhile, McPherson advanced from Decatur parallel to the line of the railroad, skirmishing heavily as he went along. Hood sent a small force in an effort to slow him but to no avail. His troops advanced so fast that by three o'clock on the twenty-first of July his army fell upon the first line of earthworks guarding Atlanta and captured it; before nightfall, he gained a high position on Bald Hill overlooking Atlanta. McPherson sent the following report to Sherman:

> In the Field, July 21, 1864.
> 3 P.M.
>
> Brigadier General Leggett, commanding Third Division, 17th Corps, advanced his lines and captured a hill, quite a commanding position, this forenoon. General Leggett is on my extreme left. The hill is two and one-fourth miles from Atlanta and a portion of the enemy's works around the town are in view. The enemy made one vigorous assault and two feeble attempts to recapture the hill but were signally repulsed. Since then, he has been moving troops in the direction of our left. General Leggett reported having seen at least ten regiments passing in that direction. I have strengthened that portion of the line with all the available troops I have got.
>
> I will remark in closing that I have no cavalry as a body of observation on my flank; and that the whole rebel army, except Georgia Militia, is not in front of the Army of the Cumberland.
>
> Very respectfully,
> JAS. B. MCPHERSON, MAJ. GENERAL

This is one of the last reports from McPherson to Sherman.

General Sherman states in his *Memoirs* that on the twentieth he had sent the whole of Garrard's division of cavalry thirty miles east to destroy two important bridges, with orders to be gone four days. McPherson, therefore, had no cavalry to guard his left flank, or to keep him apprised of the enemy's movements.

It is difficult to understand Sherman's ordering all of the

cavalry so far away at such a critical time. It was said that Sherman did not approve of so many horses, saying that a horse needs ten times as much food as a man; that the amount of forage needed for them occupied too many railroad cars and wagons, and interfered with rapid movements.

Regardless of the element of truth in those ideas, cavalry was an essential in warfare of that time. This was the second time in the Atlanta campaign that McPherson's need of cavalry was great, indeed.

On the night of the twenty-first of July, Hood sent Hardee with four divisions far to the south and around McPherson's army. When within two miles of Decatur, he faced north and established his battle line.[2] Hood was sure of success, for he knew that Sherman's cavalry was out of the way, and apparently no Yankee had discovered the march. He rested his men for a time, then prepared for a hard fight in the morning.

On the morning of the twenty-second, the advance lines of the enemy were found empty from Bald Hill north to Thomas. This led Sherman to believe that Hood meant to evacuate the city. He, therefore, ordered a general advance. But McPherson was more prudent. He well knew the character of his old classmate, and couldn't imagine Hood's giving up Atlanta without a struggle. He ordered skirmish lines moved forward to the crest of the hills overlooking the city, and rode out to this crest to study the situation. As he looked down into the interior lines of rebel works and through the streets of the city, he could see a few men moving about. No other living object was visible. Hood, as was later learned, expected him to advance at once upon Atlanta. Sherman, too, apparently expected the same. The rest of the army, in fact, had begun to move.

The caution that McPherson had shown on other occasions asserted itself again. Knowing well Hood's aggressive nature, he doubted this sudden evacuation; he wanted to study it further before sending his army into Atlanta. He was confident that Hood's fighting had been of too short a duration for him now to give up the city for whose safety he had just been elevated. To that caution the North owed the salvation of its forces in that area. Suspecting Hood's design to attack the advancing troops from the side and rear, McPherson, after giving some general directions to Logan and Dodge to maintain their positions, rode back to General Blair's headquarters. There he was told of the appearance of rebel cavalry in the rear, threatening the hospitals.

Feeling that this justified his caution, he ordered the removal of the hospitals to a safe position. He then gave verbal orders to Dodge to move Sweeny's division to the extreme left flank; to send Fuller's First Brigade, Fourth Division to left and rear of the Seventeenth Corps (Blair); and the Second Brigade, Fourth Division, to Decatur to cover the wagon trains coming from Roswell, in the absence of Garrard's cavalry. Having thus strengthened his lines, McPherson rode away hastily to consult General Sherman in the Howard House.

On the twenty-second of July, McPherson's Army of the Tennessee lay east of Atlanta and extended south of the Augusta Railroad.[3] General Logan's Fifteenth Corps was spread across the railroad; General Blair's Seventeenth Corps (Third Division, Leggett; Fourth Division, Giles A. Smith) was at the extreme southern part. The Sixteenth Corps, General Dodge, was the reserve. It had been ordered to destroy the Augusta Railroad but had been detained by McPherson's fear of impending attack.

General Sweeny's division moved south of the railroad, and Fuller's First Brigade found its place in the rear of the Seventeenth Corps. If McPherson had known Hood's plan of attack, he could not have made a better disposition of his troops.

As McPherson was discussing the situation with Sherman, and while the latter was insisting there was nothing left but to march into Atlanta and take possession, they could hear the guns from Schofield's lines and from Thomas's to the right, and from McPherson's to the left. Suddenly, firing became more lively, and guns from the direction of Decatur could be heard. By noting the place from which the sounds came, they decided they were left of McPherson's position!

Hardee had made his attack!

McPherson jumped on his horse and, with his Adjutant General Clark, Inspector General Strong, his aides Captains

Steele and Giles and his orderly A. J. Thomas, hurried down his lines, saying he would send word to Sherman what the new sounds meant.[4]

He found Dodge's corps in position, struggling against an unusually fierce assault; Blair's corps, which had been facing Atlanta, was holding firm, having jumped over their earthworks to face the enemy. But between the two corps there was a gap that was not yet closed, because of the sudden formation of the new line, now facing what had been their left flank. McPherson sent three of his staff members in haste to have this gap filled. As he and Strong neared what had been Dodge's left, they saw the advance of the rebels in the distance. Later, Colonel Strong described the conflict that he and McPherson witnessed together:

> The enemy, massed in columns three or four lines deep, moved out of the dense timber several hundred yards from Dodge's position and after gaining the open fields, halted and opened fire. They seemed surprised to find our infantry in line of battle prepared for attack and, after facing for a few minutes the destructive fire from the divisions of Generals Fuller and Sweeny, fell back in disorder to the cover of the woods. Here they quickly reformed and again advanced.
>
> The scene at this time was grand and impressive. It seemed to us that every mounted officer of the attacking column was riding at the front or at the left or right of the first line. The regimental colors waved in advance of the lines, and not a shot was fired by the rebel infantry although their movement was covered by a heavy fire of artillery back in the woods.
>
> It seemed impossible, however, for the enemy to face the sweeping, deadly fire from our infantry, while the guns of Laird's 14th Ohio and Welker's batteries fairly mowed great swaths in the advancing columns. They closed up the gap and preserved their order; but the iron and leaden hail poured upon them was too much for flesh and blood to stand, and before reaching

> the center of the open fields, the columns were broken and thrown into great confusion. Taking advantage of this, a portion of McPherson's forces charged them with fixed bayonets and drove them back to the woods, taking many prisoners.

After witnessing this, McPherson gave an order to Colonel Strong relating to the closing of the gap between the two divisions. He then went toward the Seventeenth Corps with only his orderly in attendance. His troops as he passed saluted him with great cheering.

The area occupied by these troops was wooded, and the road that McPherson followed was along the line of the Sixteenth Corps. It had been constantly used by the Union men but a few minutes before. As he entered the woods that stretched between the two corps, he was met by a staff officer with word that the left of the Seventeenth Corps was being pushed back by an immensely superior force of the enemy. McPherson stood for a moment or two studying the lay of the land sloping away from him, and the arrangement of troops. He then ordered the staff officer to hurry with word to General Logan to send a brigade immediately to close the gap, and showed him how to use it on its arrival. With that, he drove the spurs into his horse and rushed up the road toward the Seventeenth Corps. But already the enemy was crowding into the gap! He had gone hardly one hundred and fifty yards into the woods when he was confronted by a skirmish line of gray. A shrill cry of "Halt!" rang out as McPherson, in general's uniform, came in sight. He stopped for an instant and raised his hat, then with a quick jerk of the rein, he dashed into the woods at his right. But his native gallantry and refinement of manners occupied the time he needed to get out of the range of the rebel bullets. In that instant, the skirmishers sent a crashing volley after the escaping officer. He clung to the saddle a moment, while the horse carried him farther into the woods. He then fell to the ground, "the knightliest figure in the Union Army, and one of the most brilliant men—his letters read like a philosopher's notebook."[5]

The orderly played dead as the rebels stripped the general

of his watch, sword belt, field glasses and his pocketbook, which contained orders from Sherman. All of these articles were recovered from prisoners taken during the day except his watch. No article of clothing had been taken from his person, as had been reported, except his hat; that may have been lost in the woods before he fell from his horse.

When the orderly saw the rebels driven back, he left to get help. In a few minutes an advancing column of McPherson's men met a riderless horse coming out of the woods. It was wounded in two places and there were marks of three bullets on the saddle. All recognized it as the horse of their beloved commander. The news spread rapidly through the army that he was either captured or killed.

Shortly after, Ordnance Officer Buell and General Strong met Private George Reynolds of Company D, 15th Iowa Infantry, and Joseph Shorland of the 64th Illinois Infantry; they reported that they had just left the general's body and that he was dead. The officers immediately secured an ambulance, and the two soldiers guided them to the spot where the general's body was lying. John C. Tarris of Company G, 129th Infantry I.V.I. joined them and helped bring McPherson's body from the woods and place it in the ambulance.

George Reynolds reported that when he found the general he was still alive but unable to speak. He died very soon after. Reynolds, who was wounded, refused to have his wound dressed until the remains of the general had been secured and had arrived at General Sherman's headquarters. McPherson's orderly, A. J. Thompson, later came and told Sherman that he had gone to obtain help for his commander but when he got back the body was gone. He came at once to headquarters.

> Sherman had the body carried inside the Howard House and laid on a door wrenched from its hinges. Dr. Hewitt of the army was there and examined the wound. He concluded that McPherson must have died a few seconds after being hit; that the ball had ranged upward across the body and passed near the heart.

While the body was being examined, the battle was raging outside and many shots struck the house. Fearing that it might take fire, Sherman ordered Captains Steele and Giles to carry the body to Marietta.

General Sherman ordered the staff officer who had brought him news of McPherson's death, to return at once, find General (Black) Logan and tell him the facts; to instruct him to fight the battle with McPherson's troops, the Army of the Tennessee. Sherman was with difficulty keeping his mind on the battle, alternately receiving and writing dispatches, walking around the room, and occasionally stopping to gaze upon the face of his dead comrade, his greatest support. It was a trying time for him, wondering how affairs were going in the field with General Logan[6].

The news of the tragedy spread along the lines and the soldiers voiced their grief and despair in shouts of "McPherson! McPherson!" That cry arose above the din of battle and, as it ran onward, swelled in power until the roll of musketry and the booming of cannon seemed drowned in its frenzy. Logan's face was pale, his black eyes appeared to burn, and his long black hair flowed in the wind as he rode up and down the battle line, rallying his men.

The enemy attacked fiercely and repeatedly all along the front, for Hood knew that the fate of the Confederacy would be decided by this "Battle of Atlanta." He sent wave after wave of men into that carnage. They were met by equally grim determination and fierce resistance; and on that ground Hood's men and McPherson's Tennessee battled far into the night.

After dark, Logan wrote to Sherman:[7]

Every wave of Rebel troops was thrown back. The shout of rebels confident of victory was drowned by the battle cry of "McPherson" which went up from the Tennessee. In the late afternoon, the enemy made a fierce attack on the Fourth Division of the Seventeenth Corps. His assault was described by the officers engaged as the

> fiercest and most persistent engagement of the day.
>
> The enemy moved in through the woods at some points within three feet of our breastworks. Under a most destructive fire from the Fourth Division and two detached regiments of the Third Division, the enemy moved up directly to our works and a deadly battle took place. Regimental commanders with their colors, and with such men as would follow them, often would occupy one side of the works and our men the other. The flags of opposing regiments would be flaunted by their respective bearers in each others' faces; men were bayoneted across the works, and officers with their swords fought hand to hand with men with bayonets. The Colonel of the 45th Alabama was pulled by his coat collar over the works and made a prisoner. This terrible contest lasted an hour, but the Division still held nearly the whole ground.
>
> About seven o'clock another force advanced from the direction of Atlanta. Another severe attack by the enemy in their determination to gain Bald Hill was met by the Seventeenth Corps who fought with wild desperation to hold their ground. The battle closed long after dark and our troops held the field. The enemy retired in the night after removing the greater part of their wounded. Their dead were left on the field.

Logan's second report to Sherman said that his total loss in killed, wounded and missing was 3521; also ten pieces of artillery.

> We have buried and delivered to the enemy over 5,000 dead; burying parties are still at work. We have over 1000 wounded rebels on our hands, the larger number of wounded having been carried off during the night.
>
> We captured 18 stands of colors and 5,000 stands of arms. The attack was made on our lines seven times, and as many times repulsed. We have sent to the rear 1,000

> prisoners, including 33 commissioned officers of high rank. Estimated loss to the enemy at least 10,000.

While this battle was raging, staff officers Steele and Giles with an escort were slowly taking the body of their general over the shell-gutted road to the hospital in Marietta.

The hospital, a large, rambling old house, to which Sherman had ordered McPherson's body sent, was in charge of Mother Bickerdyke, an old army field nurse, one of the many who cared for the broken boys in blue in Sherman's army after the battle on that hot July day.[8] So the young general was carried to her. She washed off the blood stains where the bullet had gone to his heart, brushed his hair, and covered his face with her finest linen. She gathered together his belongings that came with the body and packed them ready to send to his mother in Ohio. She then went outside to rest a few minutes in the cool night air.

After midnight, a man came furiously riding toward the hospital. He stopped, sprang to the ground and threw the bridle over the horse's neck. The tired nurse went to see who the visitor was.

"Why, General Logan! Is that you? What has happened?"

"Mother Bickerdyke," said the general, "is McPherson here? Is he safe? I am to report to Sherman, and I could not go without seeing McPherson once more. Show him to me."

Down through the dimly lighted room she led General Logan. Far to the end of the room lay the silent soldier. He was handsome in death. General Logan knelt down, passed his hand over the still face, and looked steadily for a few moments. He then turned away.

"Yes, he is safe with you. It will comfort Sherman, too, to know he is not alone. I may be brought to you one of these days myself."

Logan crushed his old soft hat on his head, brushed the tears from his big black eyes, and smiled into the nurse's face a wordless farewell. He then was off to report to Sherman that the dead McPherson was safe.

The next morning Generals Sherman and Logan rode along

the entire line to the left of the Howard House, and both were received with wild enthusiasm by the troops who had done such severe and splendid fighting the day before. The sight of the great number of Confederate dead in front of our lines was appalling.

Sherman said, "The army and the country have sustained a great loss by the death of McPherson. I had expected him to finish the war. Grant and I are likely to be killed or set aside after some failure to meet popular expectations, and McPherson would have come into chief command at the right time to end the war. He had no enemies."

While McPherson's body was being carried by special train to his home in Clyde, expressions of regret for his untimely death and words of appreciation of his services to his country were heard on every hand.

General Grant, who was with his army before Petersburg, retired to his tent and wept when he received the news. Later he said, "The country has lost one of its best soldiers, and I have lost my best friend."

General Hood in Atlanta stated:

> I will record the death of my classmate and boyhood friend, General James B. McPherson, the announcement of which caused me sincere sorrow. Since we had graduated in 1853, and had each been ordered off on duty in different directions, it has not been our fortune to meet. Neither the lapse of years nor the difference of sentiment which had led us to range ourselves on opposite sides in the war, had lessened my friendship; indeed, the attachment formed in early youth was strengthened by my admiration and gratitude for his conduct toward our people in the vicinity of Vicksburg. His considerate and kind treatment of them stood in bright contrast to the course pursued by many Federal officers.

The Army and Navy Journal, July, 1868, declared that "With McPherson dead, we have no heart to write exultingly of the Rebel repulse at Atlanta."

However high an estimate the leading papers of the North

had placed upon the character and genius of General McPherson, it was equaled if not surpassed by the leading rebel papers. The *Richmond Examiner* asserted that "it was his genius that had so successfully planned the reduction of Vicksburg; it was McPherson who had made Grant famous, and was about to do the same for Sherman," adding a hope that his unvaried success might breed in him a rashness that would lead to his destruction.

General Sherman, in his official report of the death of McPherson, ended with the following eulogy:

> General McPherson fell in battle, booted and spurred as the gallant knight and gentleman would wish. Not his the loss; the country and the army will mourn his death and cherish his memory as that of one who, though comparatively young, had risen by his merit and ability to the command of one of the best armies which the nation had called into existence to vindicate its honor and integrity. History tells us of but few who so blended the grace and gentleness of the friend with the dignity, courage, faith and manliness of the soldier. His public enemies, even the men who directed the fatal shot, never wrote or spoke of him without expression of marked respect. Those whom he commanded loved him even to idolatry; and I, his associate and commander, fail in words adequate to express my opinion of his great worth. I feel assured that every patriot in America on hearing this sad news, will feel a sense of personal loss; and the country generally will realize that we have lost, not only an able military leader, but a man who had he survived, was qualified to heal the national strife which has been raised by designing and ambitious men.

The body of General McPherson left Marietta July 23 and traveled north by way of Chattanooga, Nashville and Cincinnati to Clyde. A Nashville dispatch of the twenty-fifth said:

"The remains of General McPherson reached here at 9 A.M. today and were escorted through the City to the Louisville depot by the 15th Regulars, the 10th Tennessee Infantry and the 5th Regular Artillery, Generals McElroy, Webster and Gilom. Governor Johnson and Staff were in the procession which comprised all officers of the City. The remains leave by special train at 12 A.M., accompanied by a guard from the 13th Regulars of 2 officers and 50 men to Clyde, Ohio. The streets were thronged with citizens assembled to honor the remains of McPherson."

Russell McPherson, who had arrived from Memphis, was on the special which carried his brother home.

2. The News Is Received

The Soldiers Aid Society in Clyde had met with Cynthia McPherson that afternoon of Friday, July 22. In spite of the extreme heat, the ladies had sewed steadily and had finished several shirts, and cut many bandages for the "boys." Cynthia had read to them James's last letter, which told of the army's progress toward Atlanta. He had expressed hope and encouragement. After the ladies had left, Cynthia and her mother, Lydia Slocum, had their supper. As they were warm, they decided that bread and milk would satisfy them better than anything else. After partaking of it they sat on the front porch to cool themselves. They were there but a short time when Cynthia said, "Isn't that brother Norton coming this way?" Her mother looked and replied, "I wonder what brings him here this late!"

They speculated about it until he opened the white picket gate and started up the walk toward them. Cynthia noticed that his face had not the usual smile for his mother and sister.

"Something has happened," she uttered with fear in her voice. He climbed the porch steps with averted face, then looking at the two women, he tried to say something but the words would not come. Cynthia went to him, then saw the strained expression he could not hide. She cried out, "James is dead, I know he is!"[9]

Her brother put his arms around her and his mother, who had slowly made her way to him. Knowing he could not soften the news in any way he said, "Yes, Cynthia, that is what brought me here. They gave me the news from the telegraph office a little while ago and asked me to tell you." And he showed the message to the stricken women. "They are bringing him home and we must prepare for him."

Emily Hoffman's niece said, "The news arrived in Baltimore at twilight. A telegram from the Secretary of War to my grandmother notified her of the death of General McPherson and asked her to break the news to my Aunt Emily. It arrived in the late afternoon—almost dusk—when they were in the blue room together. As the lights in that room were not yet lighted, my Grandmother handed it to my Aunt Emily with the request that she read it to her. Aunt Emily took the telegram into the hall and stood under the hall lantern to read it. Suddenly my grandmother heard the sound of a falling body and rushed out to find her daughter in a dead faint with the telegram clutched in her hands."

In San Francisco the news of McPherson's death was chalked up on the bulletin boards in front of newspaper offices. Groups of his grieving friends gathered on the streets, and many called at the McLane home to discuss the virtues of their hero, "San Francisco's own" as they called him.

An article in the *Toledo Blade,* July 30, 1864, gave a full account of the funeral:

FUNERAL OF MAJOR GENERAL MCPHERSON

> The mortal remains of Major General James B. McPherson were committed to their last resting place in Clyde at one o'clock, Friday, July 29, 1864. A large crowd had assembled to witness the sad ceremonies of the occasion. . . . A pervading sadness marked the faces of those present, showing that heartfelt grief and respect had called them together. Large numbers of people arrived by cars on the "Cleveland and Toledo" and the "Sandusky, Dayton and Cincinnati" Roads; while the greater portion came in carriages from the neighboring towns and villages.
>
> The military escort from Atlanta was in attendance, and also a detail of 30 men of the 18th Regulars who met the remains at Nashville and accompanied them to Clyde.
>
> The Pall-bearers were Captain L. M. Brooks, A.Q.M.,

Lt. Col. Harmon, 171st O.N.G., Capt. N. E. Ellmaker, C.S., Maj. M. A. Fowler, 171st O.N.G., Surgeon H. Eversman, and Capt. T. Linnell, 128th O.V.I.

The corpse lay in the two-story white house, the residence of the family. Under escort of the military from the Tennessee Army, the remains were removed to the orchard back of the house where a stand had been prepared for the funeral services and where the large concourse were soon gathered. Among the mourners were Mrs. Cynthia McPherson, mother of the deceased, aged 61; the brothers, Russell B. and William McPherson, the former in the Government Railroad service at Memphis, and the latter the farmer on the homestead; the only sister, Mrs. Frederick Vandercook of Fremont; the venerable grandmother, Mrs. Lydia Slocum, aged 80 years; two uncles, Hon. William S. Russell, Probate Judge of Sandusky County and Norton Russell, retired farmer, and others more or less connected.

Prayer was offered by Rev. J. S. McCune, Chaplain of the 128th O.V.I.; after which Rev. T. F. Hilgreth, Superintendent of Sandusky County Sunday Schools delivered a discourse which was listened to with close attention. The speaker aimed chiefly to impress upon his hearers their duty as Christians, as well as citizens, to follow the bright example of the illustrious dead whose memory they had come to honor.

The remains, under military escort, were removed to an elevated point nearby which commands a fine view of the country around, and which had been selected as the end of life's journey of the one who but a few years before had been born in a log cabin a short distance away. The sad rites were closed by three charges of musketry from the 128th Regiment which was drawn up in double column near the grave. This was about one o'clock, just one week from the hour when the gallant leader of the Tennessee Army fell at the head of his loved and loving command.

Appendix

From the Wilmer Hoffman Collection:

Headquarters, Military Division of Miss.
In the field near Atlanta, Ga. Aug. 5, 1864.

Miss Emily Hoffman,
Baltimore, Md.

My Dear Young Lady

A letter from your mother to Gen. Barry on my staff reminds me that I owe you heartfelt sympathy and a sacred duty of recording the fame of one of our Country's brightest and most glorious characters. I yield to none on earth but yourself the right to excel me in lamentations for our dead hero. Better the bride of McPherson dead than the wife of the richest merchant of Baltimore.

Why, oh why, should death's darts reach the young and brilliant instead of older men who could have been spared better! Nothing that I could record will elevate him more in your mind's memory; but I could tell you many things that would form a bright halo about his image. We were more closely associated than any other men in this life. I knew him before you did. When he was a lieutenant of Engineers in New York, we occupied rooms in the same house. Again we met in St. Louis almost at the outset of this un-natural war and from that day to this we have been closely associated.

I see him now, so handsome, so smiling on his fine black horse, booted and spurred, with his easy seat, the impersonation of the gallant knight. We were at Shiloh together, at Oxford, at Corinth, at Jackson, at Vicksburg, at Meridian, and on this campaign. He had left me but a few minutes to place some of his troops in position, and went through the woods by the same road he had come, and must have encountered the skirmish line of the rebels which had made a circuit around the flank of Blair's troops. Though always active in person, amongst dangers to his appropriate duties, on this occasion he was not exposing himself. He rode over ground he had twice passed that same day, on which hundreds also had passed, by a narrow road to the rear of his established line.

He had not gone from me half an hour before Colonel Clark of his staff rode up to me and reported that McPherson was dead or a prisoner in the hands of the enemy. He described that he had entered this road but a short distance in the woods, some sixty yards ahead of his staff and orderlies, when a loud volley of muskets was heard and in an instant, his fine black horse came out with two wounds and riderless. Very shortly thereafter other members of his staff came to me with his body in an ambulance. We carried it to a house and laid it on a large table and examined the body. A bullet wound high up on the right breast was all that disfigured his person. All else was as he left me, save his watch and purse were gone.

All this time the battle was raging hot and fierce quite near us and lest it should become necessary to burn the house in which we were, I directed his personal staff to convey the body to Marietta and then north to his family. I think he could not have lived three minutes after the fatal shot. He fell from his horse within ten yards of the path or road along which he was riding. I think others will give you more detailed accounts of the attending circumstances. I enclose you a copy of my official letter announcing his death.

The lives of a thousand men such as Davis and Young and Tooms and Floyd and Buckner and Loring would not atone for that of McPherson. But so it is in this world. Some men by falsehood and agitation raise the storm which falls upon the young and honorable who become involved in its circle.

Though the cannon booms now and the angry rattle of musketry tells me that I also will likely pay the same penalty, yet while life lasts I will delight in the memory of that bright particular star which has gone before to prepare the way for us more hardened sinners who must struggle on to the end.

With affection and respect,
W. T. SHERMAN

From the Eula McConnell Baumann Collection:

To General Grant.
DEAR SIR,

I hope you will pardon me for troubling you with the perusal of these few lines from the trembling hand of the aged Grandma of our beloved General James B. McPherson who fell in battle. When it was announced at the funeral that when General Grant heard of his death he went into his tent and wept like a child, my heart went out in thanks to you for the interest you manifested in him while he was with you. I have watched his progress from infancy up. In childhood he was obedient and kind; in manhood, interesting and persevering, looking to the wants of others.

Since he entered the war, others can appreciate his worth more than I can. When it was announced to us by telegraph that our loved one had fallen, our hearts were almost rent asunder; but when we heard the Commander-in-chief could weep with us, we felt, sir, that you have been as a father to him.

I wish to inform you that his remains were conducted by a kind guard to the very parlor where he spent a cheerful evening in 1861 with his widowed mother, two brothers, an only sister, and his aged grandmother who is now trying to write. In the morning he took his leave at 6 o'clock, little dreaming he should fall by a ball from the enemy.

His funeral services were conducted in his mother's orchard where his youthful feet had often pressed the soil to gather the falling fruit. His remains are resting scarce half a mile from the place of his birth. The grave, no doubt will be marked so that passers-by will stop and drop a tear over the dear departed.

And now, dear friend, a few lines from you would be gratefully received by the afflicted friends. I pray that the God of battles be with you till rebellion shall cease, the Union restored, and the old Flag wave over our entire land.

With much respect, I remain your friend,

Lydia Slocum,

Aged 87 years and 4 months.

Headquarters, Armies of the U.S.,
Camp Point, Va., Aug. 10, 1864.

Mrs. Lydia Slocum.

My Dear Madam,

Your very welcome letter of the 3d instant has reached me. I am glad to know that the relatives of the lamented Major General McPherson are aware of the more than friendship existing between him and myself. A Nation grieves at the loss of one so dear to a Nation's cause. It is a selfish grief because the Nation had more to expect from him than from almost any one living. I join in this selfish grief and add the grief of personal love for the departed.

He formed for some time one of my military family; I knew him well—to know him was to love. It may be some consolation to you, his aged grandmother, to know that every officer and every soldier who served under your grandson felt the highest reverence for his patriotism, his zeal, his almost unequaled ability, his amiability, and all the manly virtues that can adorn a commander. Your bereavement is great but cannot exceed mine.

Yours truly,

U. S. Grant

Before Atlanta, Aug. 21, 1864.

Mrs. Cynthia McPherson.

My Dear Madam,

I have just learned through the kindness of Capt. Steele your address, and also that you desired photographs of the staff members of our late beloved Commander and your beloved son. I cannot allow this opportunity to pass without writing you a brief epistle and telling you how much I loved your noble, gallant son. I was a member of the General's staff from the 13th of December, 1862, and was with him on every skirmish and engagement from that time, and I know that he trusted me. During our stay in Vicksburg I had the honor to be a member of his private mess, and I look back to those months as the happiest portion of my life. Every person loved the General, but he was more than loved by the officers and men of the Army. All had such confidence in his judgment and discretion. And when the storm of battle came and the orders were to charge, to carry a battery or line of rifle pits, to storm a position or to hold one, every private in the ranks knew that McPherson was near—that his keen searching eye was watching them, and that he shared the dangers of the battle with them.

I have the honor to enclose a photograph of myself; also an account of the General's death which is correct in every particular. I did not leave the General's side on the 22d until he sent me with an order to Gen. Logan, not more than three minutes prior to the fatal shot.

Every member of the General's staff wishes to be kindly remembered to you and yours, and join me in heartfelt sympathy for your great loss. They will write you and send photographs. If you have some little souvenir of the General's that you could part with—some trifling article—I would be very grateful for it. I have nothing of his. Should I live to see this campaign through, I shall most certainly visit you. I know your son Russell very well, have met him often. When you write to him or see him, remember me kindly.

May our Heavenly Father guard and protect, watch and keep you safely. With the kindest regards, I remain

WM. E. STRONG, LIEUT. COL.
Army of the Tennessee.

Col. Wm. E. Strong.
DEAR SIR,

Your excellent letter, overflowing with noble sympathy, reached us some time ago. And while our tears flowed afresh at its perusal, we felt that almost another son was given us, so true, so deep, so earnest were your eulogies of the dear departed. Yes, James loved his brother Generals. The members of his staff were particularly dear to him. His whole soul was bound up in the interests of his beloved country, and he was proud of everyone who rallied to the defense of our insulted Flag.

I would have answered your letter sooner but my son Russell was going to the front, and I had hoped that you would have returned with him to our humble home. We shall be glad to welcome you, to have you sit by our fireside and at our table, and tell us of your toils, your sufferings and your triumphs.

Perhaps, with us, you would like to look over James's numerous letters breathing patriotism in every line. From the time when, a little boy, he would call me out in the grove near our rural home to admire the neatly arranged woodpiles he had cut with his little ax, till the time I carefully brushed his mended clothes, braided him a summer hat and, with earnest prayers in his behalf, let him go away awhile as clerk in a store; then a carefully planned term or two at a distant academy (poor boy, how his soul thirsted for knowledge we were too poor to give him) and thus struggling on till at the age of twenty he was kindly admitted into our great National Military Academy at West Point; all along as year succeeded year, I felt that he was becoming more and more dear to us; and yet we hardly knew why he was led, evidently, so directly in a military path.

As his studies progressed, his love for Country and zeal for her honor increased. I knew he belonged to her; and when he graduated I rejoiced to find gratitude mingled with his zeal. But when the waves of rebellion arose like giant billows threatening to deluge all our land, I felt he was mine no longer. I must give him to his Country forever, and yet, I did hope and pray that he might live. But thanks to God, if he must die, he died at the front of duty. He never did dishonor our glorious standard. He never raised a rebellious hand against the best government in the world.

He wrote me only last spring that, if need be, he would willingly give his life for his periled Country. God has accepted the sacrifice and we trust, with thousands of others of like zeal and patriotism who like him have fallen, he is now in a land where war and pain and death can never come.

Would that I had words to express my gratitude to General Sherman, General Grant, The Governor of Ohio, the members of his staff, the kindly escort, and every soldier and every citizen who honored him. How tenderly and kindly they bore him home, tearful mourners greeting them all the way. How quiet and yet how constant and manly their attentions. Was there ever such a country? Was there ever such an army? Brave heroes! In coming years how bright will be the luster of their glorious deeds!

I received your photograph which I shall carefully cherish. I have also those of the members of his staff who came with him and would like the others that his military family may be complete. We have many choice mementos or keepsakes of our dear son, and something you shall surely have.

Many thanks for your kind letter. Sympathy in our bereavement is very precious; yet I weep daily, and I believe I shall go to my grave weeping for my son. It is so hard to think we cannot have him here to enjoy domestic life when this cruel war is over. Please write again to

Your grateful but afflicted friend,
CYNTHIA MCPHERSON

P.S. We will cordially greet any of James's friends, civil or military, who may call on us.

Galt House, Louisville, Sept. 22, 1864.

DEAR MOTHER,

I have just returned from Atlanta very much fatigued but safe and sound. I did not, however, succeed in obtaining any information in regard to James's effects. . . . I went over the battlefield of the 22d of July and picked a few wild flowers and evergreens from the fatal spot where he fell. Some of these I enclose together with a copy of Genl. Sherman's report to the War Department of James's death. I also send you some verses composed by Dr. Duncan which, though perhaps not possessing any particular merit in a literary point of view, were designed to express the feelings of love and respect which the whole Army—Officers and soldiers—entertained for him. . . .

My love to all at home.
Yours affectionately,
Russ

The following extracts are from a poem written after the battle of Atlanta by Grace Duffie Boylan. The poem was popular with the Army of the Tennessee:

LOGAN AT ATLANTA

Were you there to hear on that fateful day
When Logan stopped in his gallop to say—
As he swung his hat in the July air
And carried the words to his troopers there?—
"McPherson and Revenge!"

With the roar of a lion roused to wrath
He shook the wavering lines in the path,
A god of battle as fierce as the flame
That burst from the bellowing guns as he came—
"McPherson and Revenge!"

What matter to us if the stirring shout
Met death on our lips as it hurried out,
While grape and canister, minie and shell
Pinged to the tune of that terrible yell—
"McPherson and Revenge!"

A spirit of war, a sight to inspire
Was Logan himself. With glance flashing fire,
His black mane unloosed, his bridle arm free
He rallied the hosts of the Tennessee—
"McPherson and Revenge!"

Russell McPherson returned from Atlanta in September, 1864, and spent some time in arranging James's affairs. Then he returned to Memphis and resumed his position as assistant superintendent of railroads. He remained there till the close of the war in 1865. After that he was stationed in Indianapolis in charge of the Merchants Express Company.

The following account is by Harriet Hoffman Lord:

My father said that when the news of the General's death reached my Aunt Emily she shut herself up in a darkened room and refused to eat or speak for weeks. One of her sisters, my Aunt Dora, is supposed to have ruined her eyesight by trying to read the Bible to her in the darkened room during that period. I was a little girl when Aunt Emily died but I remember her perfectly. She always wore deep mourning. . . . Of course to me Aunt Emily always seemed an old lady. She was 57 when she died. I suppose she had been a pretty girl for she was small-boned with a straight little figure and very blue eyes. Her hair was snow white and plentiful and her features were regular. She died June 15, 1891, and is buried in the family lot in Green Mound Cemetery, Baltimore. . . . When the government sent Aunt Emily the sword belonging to General McPherson after his death, her mother refused to allow her to hang it on the wall of her room.

The sword mentioned above is supposed to have been the one presented to McPherson by his officers and men in the Mississippi Campaign, and it eventually found its way to West Point.

~ ~ ~

Emily Hoffman made the trip to Clyde from Baltimore on at least one occasion and visited Cynthia McPherson. Margaret Adare wrote:

"I remember seeing Emily Hoffman who visited Clyde when I was about eight years of age. She wore deep mourning that touched the ground when she walked. Everyone knew that she had been General McPherson's fiancée.

In the late 1860's Cynthia McPherson sold the house on the corner of Maumee Pike and Maple Street. Billy, Mattie and little Jimmie, who had been living there, moved into the frame house on the McPherson farm at the corner of the pike and the Bradford Road. Billy had the care of James's black horse, which had been sent north after the general's death. Cynthia and Billy were fond of it and gave it the best of care. On March 22, 1871, while Billy was currying it, it suddenly kicked and struck him on the head, rendering him unconscious. He remained in that condition for about twenty-four hours and died the next morning. Later, Mattie and her boy moved to a house owned by Cynthia on East Street.

After the death of Billy, Russell McPherson resigned his position in Indianapolis and came home to stay. On April 17, 1871, he was appointed postmaster in Clyde. Cynthia McPherson rented her farmland, and she and Russ lived in the home.

The general's horse was taken to Fremont and placed in the care of Mr. and Mrs. Nathan Birdseye, who had moved from Birdseye's Corners to the corner of Maumee Pike and Buchanan Street in that city after their daughter Cornelia and family had made Fremont their home. The horse lived a life of ease and died of old age.

~ ~ ~

Lydia Slocum continued to live alternately with her children, Cynthia, William and Norton. On October 4, 1876, Mrs. Slocum passed away at the age of ninety-nine years.

On the third of March, 1875, Russell McPherson retired from his position as postmaster, because of failing health. He passed away on February 27, 1877. He never married.

Cynthia Russell McPherson passed away at her home on the Maumee Pike on Sunday morning, May 6, 1883, at the age of 77 years, seven months and twenty-six days. She had suffered an attack of malarial fever in March which had left her in a weakened condition from which she had failed to rally. Her remains were carried to McPherson Cemetery and placed beside those of her husband, William, and near to those of her three sons, James, Russel and Billy.

Emeline McPherson Vandercook, wife of Frederick R. Vandercook, departed this life on April 17, 1884. She was aged fifty-four years, three months and eleven days. The only daughter of William and Cynthia McPherson, she was the last surviving member of her family. She left three children, Mrs. Emma McConnell, Frederick, Jr., and Eula Vandercook. Her remains rest in the McPherson burial lot on the beautiful knoll near the monument of her illustrious brother, Major General James B. McPherson.

Effort to Move the General's Body to Washington

The following was taken from the Clyde newspaper *Sentinel* of June 17, 1876:

Last Friday evening two men arrived here from Washington and on Saturday procured the services of several men and proceeded at once to tear up the stone work of the foundation for the monument of General McPherson which was to be erected there. They had not proceeded far before they were asked to desist by U. B. Lemmon and Henry Nichols, cemetery trustees, which they did. It appeared that they entered the cemetery and commenced work without the permission of the trustees or anyone else. They had no right to do this although they had the papers to show that they had been sent for the remains. They say they were not aware that the "McPherson Monumental Association" existed nor that the Association had spent $1500 for the laying of said foundation.

The men were taken before Mayor Zelotes Perrin and, during the interview, one of the Washington men said, "General McPherson owed it to his country to be buried in Washington." Mayor Perrin replied, "Sir, General McPherson paid that debt. He gave his life for his country."

On Monday morning suit was brought against the Washington men by the cemetery trustees to recover damages to the amount of $300 for entering the cemetery without first obtaining their permission. The trial is to come off Saturday.

Since then we have learned that Captain Charles Dirlam went to Cincinnati to confer with some of the officers of the Army of the Tennessee in regard to the moving of the remains of General McPherson from Clyde to Washington, and returns with the good news that they shall not be removed. He was assured that some steps will shortly be taken for the erection of a monument on the base already laid over the mortal remains of this much loved and gallant soldier.

McPherson's Monument in Washington

An equestrian statue of Major General McPherson was erected in the city of Washington, and the cite provided by Congress and known as McPherson Square is beautifully located less than three blocks from the White House. *The National Republican,* published in Washington, D. C., October 19, 1876, gives the following account of its erection and unveiling:

HONOR TO GENERAL MCPHERSON

The Society of the Army of the Tennessee held its reunion yesterday in Lincoln Hall; General Sherman, president, presided. A holiday had been declared for the unveiling of the memorial to McPherson's memory. . . .

The procession to McPherson Square began at one o'clock. Thousands of Veterans, bands and mounted police marched from Lincoln Hall up Ninth Street to G, to Fifteenth, to Pennsylvania Avenue to the east gate of the White House grounds, passing the Executive Mansion where they were reviewed by President Grant; out of the West gate through Sixteenth and a half Street to H, east to Vermont Avenue, thence north to McPherson Square. The outpouring of people was general and the crowd was so great that the procession only with the aid of police was able to enter the square.

A stand was erected a few yards to the west of the monument, and President Grant and members of his cabinet, General Sherman and his staff, and other distinguished officers and invited guests were seated there. . . . General Sherman presided and Rev. Mr. McCarty, a retired Chaplain of the Army, invoked Divine blessing, and a religious air was played by the band. General Hickenlooper of the monument committee was introduced by Gen. Sherman and gave a report on the business of securing funds, etc. for the monument. He said, "We desire to return our sincere thanks to our comrades of the Army of the Tennessee who have so generously contributed their time and money to this undertaking; to Francis Skidde and Louis McLane for their magnificent and cheerfully bestowed contributions; to the artist, Louis Rebisso for his unparalleled devotion to the work entrusted to his care; to Congress who by their wise and liberal legislation have made it possible for us to locate within the National Capital this statue of a nation's hero. . . .

And now, General Logan, with thanks to you personally for the thought which prompted its execution, we transfer to your care a statue significant of the unparalleled heroism, chivalric daring, unselfish patriotism and gentle demeanor of our loved and lamented commander, Major General James B. McPherson."

The statue was then unveiled amid cheers and shouts from the crowd and it was several minutes before order was restored. General Sherman then introduced the orator of the day, Major General John A. Logan, who delivered an oration which was received with enthusiasm and applause. General Logan, McPherson's most trusted division commander, in a two-hour discourse traced the rise of his beloved commander and most cherished friend from a small boy in Clyde, Ohio through the Military Academy at West Point, teacher at the latter place, in command of building fortifications in New York harbor, Fort Delaware, San Francisco and Alcatraz Island; then lead him through the Civil War and from one promotion to another until he reached the rank of Major General before he was thirty-five years of age. He described his brilliant leadership at Corinth, Jackson, Vicksburg, and in the Atlanta campaign where he met his death. He said, "Feeling that patriotic devotion on the battlefield alone could save the nation he gave his soul, his life to the work.

"It is, therefore, eminently proper that this monument to his memory should be erected here in our national shrine. . . . The artist in modeling the statue before us has evidently caught the inspiration of McPherson's presence in action, and thus has been enabled to present his graceful form as it appeared to us on so many hard-fought but victorious battlefields. . . ."

~ ~ ~

Francis B. Gessner, Washington correspondent, wrote in one of his letters to the *Toledo Blade* in 1885:

Speaking of statues in Washington, Ohio is represented by McPherson and Garfield. The McPherson statue is equestrian and stands facing the home of John R. McLean. It looks down Vermont Avenue into the doorway of the White House. Had McPherson lived he would undoubtedly have crossed the portals of that mansion as president. Only 35 when killed at Atlanta, he was a man of exceptional ability. It was General Sherman who wrote, "Had he lived he would have commanded all of us." He was killed at a time when his life gave great promise.

His body was taken to Clyde, Ohio, where his aged mother lived until 1883. A statue stands over his grave in Clyde and it can be seen from his mother's window. In the dark stormy days of winter the dear old mother would look out upon the bronze figure of her son and exclaim, "Oh, it seems so cold out there for my Jimmie. I ought to take out some clothes for him this cold winter day."

When McPherson died he was engaged to a young woman of Baltimore. After his statue was erected here, that young woman came to Washington once a month and sat for an hour in silent contemplation of his heroic figure.

The McPherson Statue in Clyde, Ohio

The statue that the Army of the Tennessee had decided to erect over the remains of Major General McPherson in Clyde was unveiled on July 22, 1881, seventeen years after his death. The *Fremont Journal* gave the following account of it:

CLYDE'S DAY

The statue which is erected by the Society of the Army of the Tennessee was made at the Cincinnati Art Foundry by Louis Rebisso, one of the famous sculptors of the day, and who in 1876 executed an equestrian statue of General McPherson which was unveiled in Washington. The statue is a remarkably beautiful one, both in point of design and clearness of execution. General McPherson is represented in an upright position, with his right arm thrown gracefully forward and his head, covered with the regulation army slouch hat, thrown slightly to the left as if bidding his followers onward. In his left hand he carries a field glass, and his sword hangs by his side. The bearded face bears a most natural expression in which is depicted intense ardor and determination.

Clyde today is the center to which all the patriotic eyes of the country are turned. Every train brings hundreds of Veterans of the War, Military companies, bands, and the masses generally. Never before has Clyde known such a crush. The decorations along the line of march are handsome and abundant. The Sixteenth Regiment, O.N.G. went into camp on the Clyde Fairgrounds Tuesday. The Cleveland Grays, Toledo Cadets, Tiffin Zouaves, and the Governor's Guards of Columbus will be present. Over twenty Posts of the Grand Army of the Republic, most of them accompanied by bands, will be present: People are coming all the time, among the number being a party of 800 from Bloomington, Illinois and a group of 200 from Iowa.

The official program of the exercises of the day is as follows:

National Salute at sunrise by Captain O. F. Hopkins, Fourth Ohio Battery.

The morning until 12 o'clock will be devoted to receiving delegations and guests.

Dinner throughout town will be served at 10:30 A.M.

The procession will be formed at 1 P.M. and will move promptly at 1:30 directly to McPherson's Cemetery where the assemblage will be called to order by ex-President Hayes. The following exercises will take place:

1. Prayer by Rev. Robert McCune, Chaplain 16th Regt. O.N.G.
2. Unveiling of the statue by Gen. W. T. Sherman
3. Song, "America"
4. Oration by Maj. Gen. M. F. Force of Cincinnati
5. Song, "Marching Through Georgia"
6. Address by Gen. W. E. Strong of Chicago
7. Song, "Sherman's March to the Sea"
8. Short addresses by Generals Sherman, Logan, Gibson, Leggett, Belknap, Governor Foster and others
9. Singing of Doxology and Benediction, Rev. J. S. Brownell

The exercises will be concluded at 5 P.M.

Grand Marshall, General Buckland, assisted by Col. W. C. LeFever

NOTES

The grandstand has been erected in the center of the Western Reserve and Maumee Pike, fronting the cemetery. Its dimensions are 32 by 60 ft. The speakers of the day and invited guests will occupy the center and the newspaper men at either end.

Several handsome arches of evergreens and flags span the streets. Over fifty newspaper men were present.

The local editor of the *Journal* is indebted to H. L. Paden of the *Enterprise and Sentinel* for much information and courtesy.

Twenty special police.

A male quartette composed of A. J. Wilder, C. Hunter, H. W. Miller and E. E. Hall will lead the singing. A. D. Ames will be organist.

Bellevue and Fremont will come to Clyde "en masse" and business places will be closed.

Refreshment stands and eating places are everywhere, and people find plenty to eat.

Notes, July 29, 1881 (Fremont Journal)

We doubt if any military hero ever received, as worthily, such high encomiums of praise as were accorded to General

McPherson on the occasion of the unveiling of the statue erected to his memory.

Number of people in attendance was estimated to be from 15,000 to 20,000. Thousands of veterans of the late war were present, mostly from the Army of the Tennessee.

Governor Foster and Staff arrived on the train from the east about 10 o'clock.

The veterans were enthusiastic in greeting General Sherman.

It was 3 o'clock when General Sherman grasped the cords which held in place the Stars and Stripes, and unveiled to the upward gaze of thousands of eager eyes the brilliantly shining bronze figure of the beloved General, with the clear cut features so well known to the "boys." Every hat was raised and there was an instant of breathless silence, followed by a burst of applause that made the air resound. The Barrack's Band of Columbus played and Hopkins's Battery thundered forth a Major General's salute.

On the stage were the venerable mother of the hero, his sister Mrs. Fred Vandercook of Angola, Ind., the speakers of the day, and dozens of famous Generals and noted citizens of the United States.

General R. B. Hayes read a letter from President Garfield dated June 22d saying he would, unless something occurred to prevent, be present at the unveiling. [President Garfield was shot on July 2.] A telegram dated July 22 also was read from President Garfield, presenting his cordial greetings to his comrades and friends assembled in Clyde.

By unanimous vote of the assemblage, a dispatch was sent to the President congratulating him on his [apparent] gain in health and strength. "The prayer of all who are assembled here is 'God grant to our President restored health, and a long honored and useful life.'" R. B. Hayes, President of the day.

The following extracts of some of the speeches made at the unveiling of the monument in Clyde, Ohio, are taken from newspaper clippings in the scrapbook of Mrs. Baumann's grandmother, Emeline McPherson Vandercook:

Ex-President R. B. Hayes:

McPherson was in command of the Army of the Tennessee which consisted of the 15th, 16th and 17th Army Corps, and formed the left wing of the forces of General Sherman which was then in almost daily battle for the possession of strongholds and communications upon which the life of the Confederacy depended.

General Manning F. Force:

McPherson was dead. When that bright light went out the Army of the Tennessee was plunged into gloom and a shadow went over the land. Grant and Sherman wept. His staff, the most united, harmonious and loyal military family in all the Armies, were pierced with grief that the lapse of years has not dulled. He had tasted the sweets of fame without touching the dregs. He had received the grateful applause of the Nation and did not live to encounter unfounded jealousy, and baseless detraction. The sharp discipline of the Civil War had developed and exalted his character.

He had a quick and clear intelligence and an industry that never flagged. No detail escaped his vigilance. He was prudent and cautious, sometimes, perhaps, to a fault. He was deliberate in forming plans, and resolute and dashing in executing them.

Grant called him one of the ablest Engineers and most skilful Generals, and said, "The Nation had more to expect from him than from almost anyone living."

Gen. W. E. Strong of McPherson's staff:

There is no recollection in my life so sacred, so tender, so beautiful as those that lie garnered in my heart of James B. McPherson. He was my friend of friends and I loved him as I have never loved another man.

It is General McPherson's greatest praise that he was the highest type of representative of his Nation and of our Army. I speak now of the Army of the Tennessee which he commanded July 22, 1864, and which he loved to idolatry. The soldier of that Army with the experience of a thousand marches and a hundred fights, with Donelson, Shiloh, Vicksburg, Mission Ridge upon his banner, with hope to end the war, to give freedom and peace to his country, this man was there on that July morning. He had slept on the ground during the night, he had had his coffee, his hard bread and his pork for breakfast, he was now ready to do his full duty. Of this ideal American soldier James B. McPherson was the highest embodiment.

General Sherman:

My young hero lies buried here in Clyde, Ohio, in the orchard where he played as a boy. You, his neighbors, knew him as a boy, and had glimpses of him in manhood. But, somehow I think a man may not be a prophet or a hero in his own home. You knew his genial, hearty nature, his attachment to his family and his neighbors; but you could not see the man as I have seen him in danger; in battle when every muscle and every tissue was in action; when the heroic qualities shone out as a star in the darkest night. I believe I knew McPherson better than any of you, and of this I must testify.

In September 1857, I was in New York City, a citizen, agent for certain bankers of St. Louis. I found my friend, Major John Barnard, United States Engineers, quartered in a house on Prince Street not far from Broadway, and to be near him, I took rooms there. In that same house I found Lieut. McPherson of the Engineer Corps of the Army. We were usually out during the daytime but every night we met in Barnard's room or mine and gossiped about the topics of interest of the day.

I was naturally attracted to him because of his intelligence, his manly bearing and because he was from Ohio and had graduated at the head of his class at West Point. There it was our first acquaintance began, and it continued without interruption until I saw him last alive at the Howard House near Atlanta, Georgia, whence I sent his body home to Clyde for burial.

There must be many people here—I know there is one, Gen. R. P. Buckland—who remembered how intimate and friendly we were before the battle of Shiloh as well as after it. McPherson always stayed in my camp and never failed to visit the 72d Ohio belonging to my Division in which Regiment he had many old neighbors and friends from this same town of Clyde.

Before the battle of Shiloh, McPherson and I separately and together, reconnoitered all the ground to the front for twelve miles to the right and left; and when the battle of Shiloh was in progress General Grant relied chiefly on McPherson for the topographical knowledge of the battlefield and its surroundings.

Events followed each other in such quick succession that at this distance of time all seem projected in one grand result; but the years 1863 and 1864 were big with events which will influence the destiny of America for centuries to come.

McPherson, a youth, grew from a Lieutenant of Engineers to be a Corps Commander, an Army Commander, promotion as rapid as ever marked the progress of the mighty men in the days of Napoleon but, like a brilliant meteor, his young life went out before we had achieved the full measure of the work demanded of us by the times. The artist may model his form, the painter may produce his likeness, and the historian narrate his deeds; but none save his comrades in battle can feel the full force of his living genius and character.

I have sought elsewhere for words fitted to the subject, but cannot find anything more appropriate than what I myself wrote the day after his death, when the sounds of battle still thundered in my hearing, when my heart was torn by the loss of a comrade and friend on whom I had leaned, in whose keeping had been the fate of one of our best armies, and whose heart's blood still stained the hand with which I wrote.

Seventeen years ago today died this young hero and above his grave has assembled this august audience representative of all parts of America, composed of men of the most exalted stations. But we miss from our circle one who had intended to be here, who had actually started on a tour designed to embrace his Alma Mater, his own home at Mentor, and this patriot shrine at Clyde; but who now lies on a bed of pain and anguish where for twenty days he has been almost within the portals of death. I mean, of course, our President, our comrade, General Garfield. Knowing from himself his purpose to assist on this occasion and his love for the memory of McPherson, I addressed a note to Colonel Rockwell on Friday last, asking the privilege of standing by his bedside, to bring direct to you even the shortest possible message of affection, and received the following answer:

Executive Mansion,
Washington, D. C., July 16, 1881.

DEAR GENERAL,

It is the unanimous decision of the attending physicians that the President must not see any strange face for some time yet. I was permitted to deliver your message to which he responded briefly and substantially as follows:

> God bless them all. Ask General Sherman to say that in my every day of pain I have thought of them, and the hope I had to have been with them. In my suffering I feel that the dear old State is behind me.

Of course his message is brief, but from his manner I know that his heart was full of feeling.

Very sincerely,
A. F. ROCKWELL

I will not mar the effect of this tribute of affection by a single word, but I am sure that from this shrine made sacred by the ashes of McPherson will arise this day a prayer that the majestic form of General Garfield, full of health, energy and life, may soon stand where we do now, and that his clarion voice will often again be heard to cheer on in the great battle of life the hosts of young heroes who have drunk inspiration at this pure fountain of patriotism.

General M. D. Leggett, 3d Division, 17th Army Corps:

I have very often heard the remark made by those who were not soldiers in the service, that the death of McPherson was not necessary; that he came to his death in consequence of unnecessary rashness; that he had placed himself in a position that was not a proper one for the commander of an army, and in consequence of that rashness he met his death. No soldier who was in the Army of the Tennessee, and no one who was present at the Battle of Atlanta on the 22d of July, 1864, would make such a suggestion. General McPherson was not out of his place. He was not a rash man. While he possessed all the dash and daring that belonged to a brave commander, he had all the coolness and the sobriety and the forethought of the most able. He had no reason to suspect the presence of the enemy in the position they held at that time. I will explain the situation.

My line was formed just at the west of a strip of very dense timber-land, and right on the east of this woodland were my headquarters. I was on the line at the time the battle opened. General Scott, who commanded a brigade under me, went back at the first appearance of the enemy to order up a regiment that was back in the timber. One of my staff officers, Captain Raymond, had also gone back and they were returning and came up the road from headquarters. Just behind them General McPherson, seeing General Scott and Captain Raymond, both of whom he knew, and knowing also that they knew how to go to where my line was, naturally followed them into the timber. He was aware that they knew the locality. He had not been in the line himself and he took them for guides to it. The same volley that killed him, killed the horse of General Scott and that of Captain Raymond, and those officers both fell into the hands of the enemy as prisoners. Hence there was neither rashness nor lack of precaution on General McPherson's part. He saw a brigade commander going directly to his brigade and, following him, he lost his life. It was not unnecessary rashness.

In that desperate battle of July 22d, I remember very distinctly the impression produced upon those around me when we heard of the death of General McPherson. It came probably within a very few minutes of its occurrence. Soldiers here remember how rapidly information of that kind would spread through the lines. It brought the feeling—our General is gone, and we, each of us, must be our own general today. I have sometimes thought that the very desperation that seemed to take possession of our hearts after we heard that he had fallen, was one of the means by which we won the battle on that day. [Applause] McPherson had a peculiar quality of being able to inspire his men. They loved him as well as respected him.

General W. W. Belknap:

The 15th Iowa Volunteers which I had the honor to command often came under McPherson's eye, and partook of the inspiration of his presence. In that battle of giants at Atlanta, 17 years ago today, it was the extreme left regiment of the 17th Corps and fought near the spot where McPherson fell. One of its men, George Reynolds, was soon by his side pressing his canteen to those quivering lips. He gathered the silent thanks of his beloved leader to himself, from the grateful eyes which had for the last time flashed in the light of the conflict.

We remember him personally when, with modest simplicity at Corinth, with his own hands and voice awakening the teamsters as the time came for the morning march. We remember his intelligent energy at Vicksburg, his patient moderation afterwards, and his resistless power; and those of us who saw him for the last time on July 20th, two days before his death, in the saddle watching with his glass from a hill the effect of bursting shells, recall that perfect development of manly beauty whose demeanor nerved the arms of the men of our advancing columns and strengthened the chorus of their cheers.

General Wm. H. Gibson:

I remember that first day at Shiloh, when death held high carnival everywhere, the first man that I met was Colonel McPherson. I, inexperienced, drew lessons from him. On the night after that awful carnage he sat by me in the tent. He was inquiring about his old neighbors in Clyde. . . .

McPherson's blood was shed not for the hope of glory or triumph. Every drop was warmed by the fire that melted four millions of fetters and lifted to God four millions of the poor.

Notes

CHAPTER I

1. Phoebe Russell Mugg in the *Clyde Enterprise.*

2. The ancestry of General McPherson's family was found through research made by Mrs. E. D. Scrogin of Miami, Florida. Her great-great-grandmother was Harriet McPherson Willcox, a cousin to the general. Mrs. Willcox and her husband, Timothy, lived in Clyde many years and were prominent among the early settlers. Both are buried in McPherson's Cemetery.

3. Facts pertaining to the McPherson and Russell families in Clyde, Ohio, were obtained from obituaries of them written by Mrs. Frances Tuttle for the *Clyde Enterprise*. Mrs. Tuttle was an intimate friend and neighbor of both families.

CHAPTER II

1. *First Journal of County Commissioners* in Sandusky County Courthouse.

2. H. Z. Williams and Brothers, *History of Sandusky County, Ohio.*

3. Purchases and sales of land by William McPherson are listed in the recorder's office, Sandusky County Courthouse.

4. Mary Porter Stevenson in the *Clyde Enterprise.*

CHAPTER III

1. Mary Porter Stevenson in the *Clyde Enterprise.*

2. Phoebe Russell Mugg in the *Clyde Enterprise.*

3. Facts obtained from E. F. Warner, former superintendent of schools in Bellevue, Ohio.

4. Phoebe Russell Mugg, *op. cit.*

CHAPTER IV

1. Facts obtained from Mary Amsden Woodward, daughter of Isaac Amsden and his wife, Cornelia Birdseye.

CHAPTER VI

1. From the collection of Katharine Smith, youngest daughter of Robert Smith of Stemtown.
2. *Ibid.*
3. Phoebe Russell Mugg in the *Clyde Enterprise.*
4. Charles Richard Williams (ed.) *Diary and Letters of Rutherford B. Hayes,* vol. 1, Ohio State Archaeological and Historical Society.
5. As told by Elijah Brownell.

CHAPTER VII

1. From the Katharine Smith collection.
2. Henry Howe, *Historical Collections of Ohio.*

CHAPTER VIII

1. From the Hayes Memorial Library collection.
2. As told by Samuel Persing, whose wife was a daughter of Judge William Russell, brother of Cynthia Russell McPherson.

CHAPTER IX

1. From the Katharine Smith collection.
2. E. F. Warner of Bellevue gave the writer the following facts about the Underground Railway station in that town: Ed Miller's livery barn, at the corner of Main Street and the county-line road, served as a refuge for runaway slaves who had come by way of Columbus and Marion. At night they were taken to Sandusky concealed in a load of hay or corn fodder, and then they were put on a boat bound for Canada.
3. Facts obtained from Mary Amsden Woodward.

CHAPTER X

1. From the Hayes Memorial Library collection.
2. Facts obtained from Mary Amsden Woodward.

CHAPTER XI

1. From the Katharine Smith collection.
2. *Ibid.*

CHAPTER XII

1. From the Katharine Smith collection.

CHAPTER XIII

1. From the material of Harriet Hoffman Lord, Emily Hoffman's niece.
2. Amelia Neville, *The Fantastic City.*

CHAPTER XV

1. As told by Harriet Hoffman Lord.

CHAPTER XVI

1. *Battles and Leaders of the Civil War,* "U. S. Grant," Vols. 3 and 4.
2. *Ibid.*
3. Whitelaw Reid, *Ohio in the War.*
4. *Ibid.*

CHAPTER XVII

1. General D. R. Keim of McPherson's staff, *U. S. Service Magazine,* October, 1864.
2. *Ibid.*
3. *Ibid.*

CHAPTER XVIII

1. Whitelaw Reid, *Ohio in the War.*

2. *Official Records of the Civil War,* Hayes Memorial Library.
3. Whitelaw Reid, *op. cit.*
4. *Ibid.*
5. *Ibid.*
6. From the Katharine Smith collection.

CHAPTER XIX

1. As told by Hariet Hoffman Lord.
2. W. T. Sherman, *Memoirs.*
3. *Ibid.*
4. Major General George W. Cullum, *Biographical Register of Officers and Cadets of the U. S. Military Academy.*
5. *U. S. Service Magazine.*
6. From the Wilmer Hoffman collection.

CHAPTER XX

1. Whitelaw Reid, *Ohio in the War.*
2. General W. T. Sherman, *Memoirs.*
3. John Fiske, *The Mississippi Valley in the Civil War.*
4. Whitelaw Reid, *op. cit.*
5. *Ibid.*
6. *Official Records of the Civil War,* Hayes Memorial Library.

CHAPTER XXI

1. Whitelaw Reid, *Ohio in the War.*
2. *Battles and Leaders of the Civil War,* Major W. H. Chamberlain.
3. Reports of Sherman's generals on the "Battle of Atlanta," July 22, 1864.
4. Major W. H. Chamberlain, *op. cit.*
5. Fletcher Pratt, *Ordeal by Fire.*
6. Sherman's *Memoirs.*

7. *Official Records of the Civil War,* Hayes Memorial Library.

8. From the *Cleveland Leader,* 1888, as told at a G.A.R. encampment, and reprinted in the *Clyde Enterprise,* 1932.

9. Phoebe Russell Mugg gave Cynthia's exact words to the writer.

Bibliography

Army and Navy Journal (1863–64). New York.

Atherton, Gertrude. *California, an Intimate History.* New York: Harper and Brothers, 1914.

———. *Golden Gate Country.* New York: Duell, Sloan and Pearce, 1945.

Banning, Kendall. *West Point Today.* New York: Funk and Wagnalls Company, 1937.

Battles and Leaders of the Civil War. 4 vols. New York: D. Appleton-Century Company, 1884–87, renewed 1912–14.

Bowen, Catherine D. *Yankee from Olympus.* Boston: Little, Brown and Company, 1944.

Brockett, L. P. and Vaugn, Mary C. *Women's Work in the Civil War.* Philadelphia: Zeigler, McCurdy and Company, 1867.

Crouse, D. E. *The Ohio Gateway.* New York: Charles Scribner's Sons, 1938.

Cullum, Major Gen. G. W. "Biographical Sketch," *Biographical Register of Officers and Cadets of United States Military Academy.* New York: Houghton Mifflin Company, 1891.

Dana, Charles. *Recollections of the Civil War.* New York: D. Appleton and Company, 1902.

Fiske, John. *The Mississippi Valley in the Civil War.* New York: Houghton Mifflin Company, 1900.

Force, Gen. Manning. *General Sherman,* New York: D. Appleton and Company, 1899.

Grant, Ulysses S. *Personal Memoirs.* New York: The Century Company, 1885.

Hood, John B. *Advance and Retreat.* Copyrighted at Washington by G. T. Beauregard for the Hood Orphan Memorial Fund of New Orleans, La., 1879.

Howard, John Tasker. *Stephen C. Foster, America's Troubadour.* New York: Thomas Crowell, 1934.

Howe, Henry. *Historical Collections of Ohio.* 2 vols. Cincinnati, Ohio: Published by State of Ohio, 1888.

Keim, Gen. Randolph. "Life and Character of Major General James B. McPherson" (October, 1864) *U. S. Service Magazine.*

Meek, Basil. *20th Century History of Sandusky County, Ohio.* Chicago: Richmond, Arnold Publishing Company, 1909.

Motley and Copeland. *The Soldier in the Civil War.* 2 vols. New York: Stanley-Brown Publishing Company, 1885.

Neville, Amelia. *The Fantastic City.* Boston: 1932. Houghton Mifflin Company, 1932.

Peters, William E. *Ohio Lands and Their History.* Athens, Ohio: W. E. Peters, 1930.

Pratt, Fletcher. *Ordeal by Fire.* New York: William Sloane Associates, Inc., 1935.

Reid, Whitelaw. *Ohio in the War.* Columbus, Ohio: Eclectic Publishing Company, 1893.

Sherman, Major Gen. W. T. *Memoirs.* New York: D. Appleton-Century Company, 1875.

The War of the Rebellion: A Compilation of the Official Records of the Union and Confederate Armies. Washington: Govern-Printing Office, 1880–1901.

Wilcox, Frank N. *Ohio Indian Trails.* Cleveland, Ohio: The Gates Press, 1933.

Williams, Chas. Richard (ed.). *Diary and Letters of Rutherford B. Hayes.* Vol. 1. Columbus, Ohio: The Ohio State Archaeological and Historical Society, 1922.

Williams, H. Z., and Bros. *History of Sandusky County, Ohio,* Cleveland: Published by Homer Everett, Esq., 1882.

Woodward, W. E. *Meet General Grant.* New York: Horace Liveright, 1928.

Works Project Administration. *San Francisco.* New York: Copyrighted by City and County of San Francisco (Published by Hastings House) 1940.

Index